COACHING THE DEFENSIVE LINE:

BY THE EXPERTS

Edited by
Earl Browning

ISBN: 1-57167-432-2

Library of Congress Catalog Card Number: 99-64112

Cover Design: Jennifer Scott

Developmental Editor: Kim Heusel

Page Layout: Kim Heusel

Front Cover Photo: Courtesy of the University of Miami

Coaches Choice Books is a division of:

Sagamore Publishing, Inc.

P.O. Box 647

Champaign, IL 61824-0647

Web Site: http://www.sagamorepub.com

Table of Contents

Chapter

Chapter 1

MULTIPLE DEFENSIVE FRONTS

John Chavis
University of Tennessee
1996

The primary objective of the defense is to get the football. That is what the offensive coaches want. There are three ways, basically, we can get the football. We can get the offense to go three downs and out, or we can create a turnover. We coach turnovers and create drills for them. The turnovers we are talking about are fumbles and interceptions. Two years ago that was the area we felt we had to improve on. This season we got 27 turnovers, which is a little more than two a game. We would like to average about three per game. The 1990 team was the best team I had been around at Tennessee. In 1990 we had 43 take-aways. We are trying to reach that level again.

We want the players to become familiar with this statement: "You are judged by your team performance—not the victory itself." Our first goal is to win the game, but we want to perform well.

These are our priorities that fall in line with our defensive philosophy:

■ We want to play with unbelievable effort. We spend as much time grading effort as we do technique. Technique is important, but I've seen players get beat because they didn't have enough effort.

■ To put the 11 best players on the field. This takes time in terms of evaluating. We have to evaluate our scheme and personnel and find out who fits where the best. One of the biggest improvements we made on our team this year was to move our best linebacker to defensive end. We felt because of our scheme we needed a guy like that at the defensive end. That was part of our philosophy about getting the 11 best on the field.

1

■ We start with speed. Speed is the name of the game. When you look around and see teams that are having great success on defense they have speed. I don't think you can coach it, but you can improve on it. We keep that fact in mind when we recruit. There may be a lot of areas you may miss on, but you can tell if a player has speed or not.

■ The team comes first. Your players have to be willing to do what it takes to make the team as good as it can be. They have to be unselfish and have a good attitude about doing what you ask them to do. The unselfish attitude can be worked on and developed. We want them to have personal goals, but those goals don't come before the success of the team.

■ We want to play aggressive attacking defense. We keep it simple and play with reckless abandon. Don't give them more to do than they can do. Don't tie their hands. I think when you look at us on film you can see what I mean.

■ Take one play at a time. We don't worry about the plays that happened before. If you have a bad play or someone has a good play against you, you can't dwell on it. We want to concentrate on the play that is coming up, not the one that happened three downs ago. We want to play that play with unbelievable effort. If the player can't give us that kind of effort, we expect him to let us know. We can get him out and give him a blow. You know if you are rushing the passer against a 300-pound lineman, you get spent. That has helped us keep our best players fresh in the fourth quarter. It has helped morale because we've got young guys who know they are going to play.

■ We want to force turnovers. Turnovers just don't happen. We had 14 the year before. This year we increased that number by 13. We are not satisfied with 27, but it was a nice improvement. We work on creating turnovers. It is part of our philosophy and we want it to be part of the players' mentality. Unless you devote some time to that, it is not going to happen. We devote that time. It has to be part of your thinking.

■ We want to force teams into making mistakes. When you are playing aggressive and they have 11 guys to account for on every play, you have a chance to cause a mistake. We are going to play a multiple scheme, but our techniques are going to be very simple. Simplicity in the techniques allows us to be multiple in our scheme.

■ Be a great tackler. Every single day we are on the practice field we have some kind of tackling whether we are in pads or not. This past spring we had a tackling circuit. To be a good tackler you have to spend some time every day.

■ We want to score on defense. We did not score the year before, and we had four scores this year. Hopefully we'll be even better in the future.

If you want to accomplish your priorities and goals there are certain things that have to be done. This is what you sell your players on. Here are the things that they have bought into:

1) They have to be in excellent playing condition. Conditioning today is a year-round thing. It is not something you do three weeks before you start fall practice. Our weight-lifting program is one of the best in the country.

2) We must eliminate mistakes and improve daily. We practice to get better each day. We want to have perfect practices. It's not going to happen, but that is what we are working for. Success breeds confidence and confidence breeds championships. There is not a better motivator than a young man feeling good about himself. I told them I won't yell and scream about mistakes. They happen. What I will yell about is effort.

3) We want great execution and second effort. We are going to be multiple in our scheme, but we are only going to ask them to learn five or six techniques at the most. At Tennessee we are not a big scheme team. We work on techniques. The thing that makes the scheme work is the technique. We are going to master the techniques.

4) We want to maintain poise and confidence at all times.

5) Have love and respect for your teammates. We play for each other. That attitude just doesn't happen. You have to work on it. We have to lead them in that direction. We are a family at Tennessee.

A statement that we have put up in our locker room means a lot to our team. "Men have fought and winners have won because of their commitment to each other." That sums up our philosophy at the University of Tennessee. I don't have all the answers, but we believe in what we do at U.T.

Let me go back to turnovers. There are three areas we want to talk about—fumbles, interceptions, and three plays and out. I think you understand fumbles and interceptions. I want to talk about the three plays and out. We want to sell our defense on going out and playing three plays and forcing a punt. To us, that is like a turnover. In games that we played well, we had up to 10 series where we went three and out.

I'm going to mention something about tackling. It can be taught and you can become better in that skill. Better athletes are better tacklers, but you can improve with drills and fundamentals. Like I said before, we don't go on the field in pads or shorts without some form of tackling. In the spring we have a tackling circuit where we spend 15 minutes a day. Here are our fundamentals for tackling:

1) Knees bent.

2) Eyes on the target.

3) Feet moving and a good base.

4) Head up and bulled neck.

5) On contact, rip the arms up and knock the ball loose.

6) Do not lead with your helmet. We want our guys to be hitters and tacklers.

Another area we spend quite a bit of time on is pursuit. Pursuit is probably the most important part of defensive football. We do it every day. It goes back to the unbelievable effort. That is the one thing that can be taught. It doesn't matter how good an athlete we have, the effort is what we must have. You don't play at Tennessee if you don't give that type of effort. Another slogan you'll find in our locker room is this. "A man's value can be measured by his distance from the football when the whistle blows." We grade effort. We want to know who is in the picture frame when the whistle blows. If there are not 11 guys in the frame there is something wrong. Obviously, on long pass plays you won't get that. Our guys get disappointed when you point out to them that they are not in the frame. You have to let your athletes know what you expect from them in pursuit to get the kind of effort you want. Pursuit, in my mind, is mental. If you want to, you can. We can create the swarm of pursuit because we work on it. Our players visualize being big play men. They believe they are going to make big plays.

Last year in spring practice we did an agility circuit after practice every single day. It was a 20-minute session of bust-your-ass drills. We didn't have a single guy complain about what we were doing. We let them know up front what we wanted to accomplish and what we had to do to get it done.

Speed is an important part of any football team. Speed can make anyone a great football coach. If you can get speed on the field, you absolutely help yourself. That is one of the first areas we start talking about when we try to get our 11 best players on the field.

When we pursue the ball at Tennessee, we take care of individual responsibility first. Defensive football is a game of angles. You have to take the proper angle to pursue the ball. Taking the correct angle allows a player to get to a ball he wouldn't have gotten to any other way. The last thing in pursuit is wanting to get there.

What happens to your team when you become a swarming defense?

1) It eliminates long touchdowns.

2) It discourages opponents.

3) It helps to cover up mistakes.

4) It will make us a great defensive football team.

5) It makes for a great gang-tackling football team.

6) It helps to create turnovers.

That is what we believe and hang our hat on at Tennessee.

I want to get to our scheme. We are basically a 4-3 football team. We start with the defensive end. He is in a 9 technique. His inside hand is down and the inside foot is back. We want the inside hand on the outside foot of the tackle. We want the inside foot to be about six inches outside the hand. That gives him a slight tilt on his alignment. The defensive tackle to the tight end is in a 3 technique with the inside hand on the outside foot of the offensive guard. He is not tilted and is in a Straight alignment. The other tackle takes a Shade alignment on the back side of the center. We take the 5 technique to the open side and align him the same way as we do the 9 technique. Our linebackers start to play with their heels at 4½ yards deep. We adjust that based on game plan and tendencies.

The whole philosophy in our defensive front is to create a push upfield. On our stance we start with a toe-to-heel relationship with our inside foot back. It took us a long time to establish this relationship. We have a visual key on the ball and should get off on the snap of the ball. We are going to attack and read on the move. We are not a read front. We attack. We are not going to run up the field and get 2 yards deep. We are going to adjust on the move. When the ball is snapped, we charge upfield and adjust on the move. Our first step is a read step and is only six to eight inches long. We want to get it back on the ground as quickly as we can. That lets us redirect more quickly. But we are not taking anything away from our momentum.

Our linebackers are angle runners and are speed guys. Our Sam last year was a former tailback. Our Will was a high school free safety. We don't want to put them in a situation where they have to match up against a 300-pound guard or tackle. We start at 4½ to 5 yards deep so we can outrun linemen.

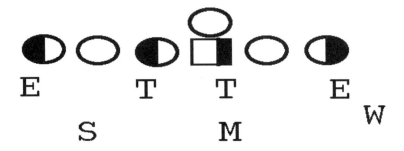

They key the backfield for run responsibility. On flow, the Sam linebacker is taught three run techniques. If he gets a down block he has a Scrap Technique. If he gets a base block, he has a Fill Technique. If he gets flow away, he has a Cut-Back Technique. We want the linebacker's feet to be about shoulders' width apart. We want to step in all directions as quickly as we possibly can. We want the heels off the ground with the weight on the inside balls of the feet. That will keep them from false stepping. We let our hands rest slightly on the knees. We want the hands to rest within the framework of the body.

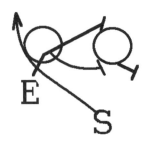

The Scrap technique is the most difficult for the Sam Linebacker to play. When he reads the down block by the tight end, our defense squeezes down inside. The Sam linebacker has to be careful that he doesn't get too wide and deep as he scraps off the defensive end's butt. He has to hug the end and get upfield.

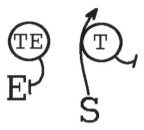

When the tight end blocks out on our defensive end, the Sam linebacker has a Fill technique. We have two ways to play this according to the scouting report. We don't want people saying they can scout us and know which way we are playing the Fill. He starts out playing outside in, keeping the outside arm free, and turning everything back into the Mike linebacker. If a team is having success running the football, he comes inside and spill, the ball outside as a change-up.

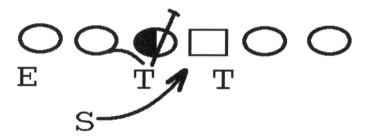

The Cutback is the last thing the Sam linebacker has to play. When Sam reads flow away, he wants to get to the inside hip of this defensive tackle to his side. We want our defensive tackle to get a push upfield. If the guard has to release quickly, the defensive tackle can be a factor in the A Gap. If the guard hangs on the defensive tackle, the Sam Linebacker gets over the top of the tackle into the A Gap. We tell him if the guard stays on the tackle he has to get across the top to the A Gap.

The Mike and Will linebackers have the same reads and techniques, except different people are blocking on them. The only difference is the Mike linebacker does not have a Cut-Back technique to play. We always tell our Mike linebacker that he is going to be on an inside-out track to the football on all run plays. The Will linebacker is in a 50 technique, which is splitting the stance of the tackle and 4½ yards deep. Our Mike linebacker is in a weak shade or 10 technique, the same distance off the football as the Will linebacker, splitting the stance of the center. Our Sam linebacker is in a 40 technique or head up the tackle and the same depth.

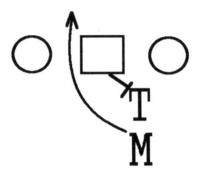

The next thing we do in our progression of teaching is to go to a G-Front. The only difference is we move the shade tackle to an inside technique on the guard. We move the Mike linebacker from a weakside 10 technique to a strongside 10. This helps us get a more balanced look and helps us on the ruboff block. The Isolation play becomes a much tougher play to run to the weak side. The 9, 5, 3 techniques, Sam and Will linebackers remain as they did in the base defense.

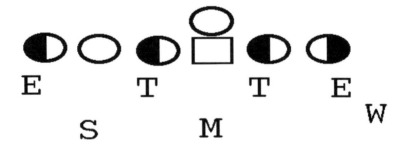

The next thing we go to is an Eagle Defense. In terms of teaching technique, there is nothing new to learn on the Eagle Defense. We have two ends in 5 techniques; our tackles are in a 3 technique and a Shade alignment. There is no new teaching for them at all. The Sam linebacker is playing a 9 technique. The reads and fills are the same as I've talked to you about before. We get into the Eagle front without any new teaching for anyone.

Out of the Eagle front we run what is called Split Defense. This is our version of the Eight-Man Front. This is the same front as the Eagle front except the Sam linebacker is declared to the split end. That puts an end in the 5 technique and the shade moves over to the 3 technique toward the split end. We have the 3 techniques toward the tight end and the end moves into a 6 or head-up technique on the tight end. That is not a new technique because that is our adjustment with two tight ends. We have to teach the Sam linebacker and strong safety something new, but everyone else is playing the same techniques. The Sam linebacker and strong safety are playing flat to curl in pass coverage. A lot of our blitz game will come off this front because we are able to disguise our three-deep and man coverage a lot better than we can from our base package.

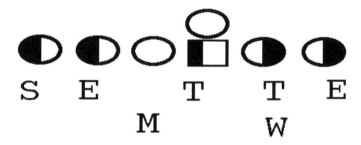

The last thing I want to show you is our Bear Front. This is a front like the Eagle and Split defense because we can stem to it. The defensive end to the tight end moves out and the Sam linebacker moves up into a 7, or inside shoulder of the tight end technique. The 3 technique and Shade tackles play the same. We could move the shade of the tackle to whatever the scouting report showed. The 5 technique end moves into the 3 technique to the split-end side, and the Will linebacker plays a loose 5 technique and becomes a pass rusher. In this situation we are usually in man-to-man coverage. The Mike linebacker is in a 3 stack with the tackle, and the Strong Safety is in a 4 technique on the tackle. This goes back to part of our philosophy. It could create a bad play for the offense. Our Bear front was very good to us this year. We moved to it 22 times during the season. On those 22 snaps the offense had minus 5 yards. It was good for us, and we probably didn't play it enough.

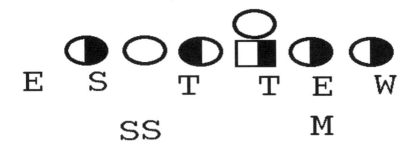

When we line up we are primarily a two-deep secondary whether we are playing quarters or halves. From our eight-man front look we do show and play some three-deep coverage. We read patterns underneath and trade route off to one another.

Chapter 2

DEFENSIVE END TECHNIQUES

Bill Conley
Ohio State University
1996

First, I want to talk about the philosophy we go by at Ohio State as it relates to End play. When I played at Ohio State we were a Slant and Angle Defense. Almost everyone in the country was running this defense, especially in the Big Ten. Then I coached the inside linebackers and we ran basically a 50 defense. Now we are a 4-3 team. Within the last few years we became a Stack 4-3 team. Now we have a little different philosophy. I learned one thing in coaching high school and college: there are certain things that do not change. I know this for sure: if you are coaching a Four-Man Front as compared to a Five-Man Front, you better be able to control things up front. If you go against a good Two-Back Attack with a Four-Man Front, you better have good people up front and some attacking linebackers. You are going to get the Isolation and the Sprint Draw run down your throat all day long. So our philosophy, especially on defensive end play, is this. Number 1, we are going to attack. To be a defensive end at Ohio State you better be physical. You better be ready to get after it. I am not saying you have to bench press the world or be one of the strongest players on the team. That comes as you develop in the weight program. The biggest difference in high school athletes coming into college is not always how fast they run, and it is not always the techniques. You can teach techniques in a short amount of time. You do have to become efficient at those techniques in college. The big thing, or difference, is the strength factor. You have to be strong to be physical.

The main thing is that you have to attack. Also, you have to give great effort to get to the football. The team must swarm to the football. The key to playing the 4-3 Front is the fact that the whole front must Attack. The second part of that is the defense must Squeeze

11

from the defensive end area. You can't play a read at the line of scrimmage with just four men. Teams can talk about read, but you must penetrate.

The next step is to React. You must learn to react on the run. What I am talking about is this: We call our end on the strong side our Leo. On the other side we call him the End. We have our Tackle and Nose inside.

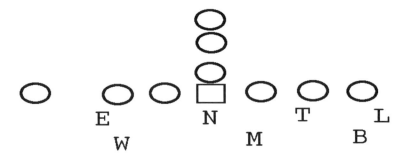

We must attack, and squeeze, forcing the ball to go east and west. The ends force the ball to go outside. If they try to run inside, we squeeze the hole. You have to play on their side of the ball. It is an attack defense. That is the key. Don't try to play a read defense with a Four-Man Front or you will get beat every time.

It does not matter what level you play on, you must stop the run first. You have to get yourself in a position where the offense has a bad situation. You want it to be second and 5 or more. You do not want it to be second and 2, or second and 3. If you do that you will be hurting for sure. Make sure you are forcing the situation to make the offense throw the ball or come up with something a little different or unique on second down. That is our basic philosophy behind our Defensive End Play at Ohio State.

Next I want to show you the Base Technique. We will talk about three basic things. We only have two techniques for ends at Ohio State. One is a Base Technique, and the other is a Rush Technique. Everything comes off those two techniques. The key to any defense at any level is Repetition, and Keep It Simple. Keep it simple so your players can be aggressive. The more you make them think, the more you increase the chance they will not be successful. If they have a lot to think about they definitely will not be aggressive. This is especially true for your people up front because things happen so much quicker. In the secondary you can react to a lot of things. Up front we want to keep it simple. All of our adjustments, with a few exceptions for our linebacker, are done with our secondary. We want to keep things basic and simple up front so our players can attack.

In our Base Technique we will talk about Stance and Alignment, Get Off (Key Man), and Reaction. First, our Defensive Ends are in a three-point stance. The inside hand is to the outside foot of the offensive man. When we get ready to line up, we want to line up on the split-end side or the tight-end side — it is all the same. They are interchangeable. The Leo lines up on the Tight End and the End lines up in a 5 technique on the split-end side.

What happens is a lot of teams like to trade the Tight End. They will start him off on one side, and shift or move him to the other side of the line after they line up. Instead of running our whole front around to the other side, we just wave at each other and switch spots because the techniques are the same. As the end, I want my inside hand to the outside foot of the offensive man. It is elongated, with the inside foot back. It is not a square stance. We are not a read technique. We are an attacking front. Our elongated stance is determined, not by the stance of the offensive man, but more by the physical makeup of each end. The tall players have even more of an elongated stance. It is the feet spread from toe to heel, and most of them will be longer than that.

Next, the butt is slightly higher than the helmet, with the inside foot back. We are in a narrow three-point stance with the butt up in the air. Next you see that we are slightly tilted with our aiming point, 1½ yards behind the offensive man's inside hip. We want to crowd the ball. What we are saying is this: Just by the nature of our alignment on the offensive man I am tilted inside in an attacking mode. We tell them they must penetrate to that 1½-yard aiming point behind the man. No matter what happens, we have to get there.

We will not be denied. If that man is in our way, we want to take him with us. We must do that.

We crowd the ball. We want to get as close to the ball as possible. The advantage we have in college is this. In high school, if a defensive lineman jumps into the neutral zone, it is a penalty. That is not the case in college. If we jump into the neutral zone we can get back and go again. When you look at the side angle, we may be lined up offside at times. But the officials do not call that a lot. Once in a while officials will call it. We just back them up for a couple of plays and then go back where we started from.

We crowd the ball as much as possible. We are in a three-point stance with our butts up in the air. When that offensive man moves, we are going to attack through him. That is what we call the GET-OFF. We want to get to that spot 1½ yards deep. Both of our Ends are coming at an angle. We are going to automatically squeeze the off-tackle hole. There is no off-tackle hole. By bringing our Ends down at an angle we knock the ball inside. The key is to have a Nose and Tackle who are knocking their men upfield. We want to knock the offensive line upfield enough to create a new line of scrimmage on the offensive side of the ball. The Ends squeezing will force the ball to go east and west.

On the Get-Off we key the man. A lot of teams key the ball. In the rush technique we do key the ball. But, if it is a running situation, where it is 50-50 that they are going to run the ball, we are going to be in a base technique, lined up in a three-point stance, and we key the man. We have a lot of individual drills that we do in our individual periods where we will move a foot or move a hand to key the defender. If the offensive man twitches, we are going to attack. If you will think about it, if you come out in an elongated stance you have a lot more power and momentum as you move. You have more power than someone that is in a wide, three-point base stance. This is because the first thing they have to do is to take a short jab step. As they take a short jab step, the offense attacks and gets into them.

We have the proper stance, and we are in the proper alignment. We are keying the man. The man moves. BOOM! What happens next? Now, we are going to talk about the different types of blocks you will face. We see the following types of blocks: Base, Down, Reach, Over-Reach, Pass Protection, Draw, and Screen Blocks. I will talk about what you will do as you attack the offense and they apply one of these blocks against the defense. I want to cover the reaction as you are attacked by these blocks.

First is the Base Block. This is the first thing you start off teaching. To the defensive man, what is the most aggressive thing the offensive man can do? It is to come off the ball and try to put his face mask in the defender's numbers and knock him off the ball. Coaching Point: Against the Base Block, we talk, coach, preach, and teach hand position. The biggest mistake the defensive man makes is to grab the blocker by the shoulder pads and fight with him. You can't do that. They let the offense hold so much today you can't fight with that man. Our hand position is very important.

As we are taking that first step, as we are replacing the hands, we are expecting the Base Block. We expect that above all. We want our hands to hit so the inside hand hits the base man's side number, and my outside hand hits the "V" right square where the armpit is to the inside. As we make contact we snap our hips and lock out. It has to be all one motion. So many players will lead with the chest and hand, and it gives the offensive man a chance to grab you. Some young players that are not as strong as some of our experienced players will make the mistake of letting the face mask get inside the same time the offensive blocker gets his hands inside. When contact is made we want a big BOOM! The hips must snap and the arms must lock out. The thumb on the hand on the number must be at one o'clock and the thumb on the hand under the armpit must be at 11 o'clock.

As we make our move against the Base Block, our feet must keep moving. You cannot stop moving your feet. We want to Lock Out as we are attacking. Remember, where did we say we wanted to end up? We want to get 1 ½ yards just inside the offensive man. The only way to get there is to keep moving your feet. Your feet have to be slightly in and the weight on the inside balls of the feet. I heard a coach describe the stance like this: "It is just like pushing your car out of the mud." The power comes when you get on the inside balls of your feet. You have to be pushing and pushing. The same is true in football. That is where your power is. If the blocker tries to Base Block me I want to create a new line of scrimmage by knocking him back off the line. Again, the advantage I have is the fact that I am coming off in a narrow, elongated stance. The blocker has to take a short jab step. By that time, BOOM! I want to be in his face. That is against the Base Block.

The next block we see is the Down Block. Here we have some real key coaching points. Our philosophy is to make the ball bounce east and west. If we get a Down Block we are going to come running off the hip. But, we must make contact. This defense is not like the 50 defense where we had to worry about keeping that man off the line-backer. That is not the way the 4-3 works. However, we must bump the blocker long enough so the linebacker can shuffle and get to where he is supposed to be. I said the first thing we are going to expect when that man comes off the ball is that he is going to base block me. As I attack the blocker he tries to go down inside. Now I have to come up fast and hard enough so I get a piece of the blocker. There is no way I can get both hands where I want them to be. My inside hand must get to the base of the inside number. I at least want to get that much of the man. Sometimes we may only get a piece of the hip. You have to practice this technique. You must knock him off his course a little. So you practice that first step with the hand coming up where you can get it in place with the thumb up. We use the Quick Draw Drill to work on this. We say from the holster to the number. BOOM! We want the thumbs up. We sprint off the butt. It is like the old roller derby, where they whip around the corner. That is what we want against the blocker.

We are going to attack anything off the hip. I start my line of vision from the center to the back. I am looking for anyone to trap or kick me out. If there is no one coming to trap or kick me out, my vision now goes to the near back. It may be the Sprint Draw or Off-Tackle play. Now I am going to take on the fullback. The only exception to that is if I have an offset fullback. Then my vision will go to him first. When the offensive lineman goes down inside we are going to come running. There is no way we should ever get trapped or kicked outside by an offensive lineman. There should be an explosion taking place at the inside hip of the near guard if the backside guard is pulling. We are checking his course as we are attacking to see if it is a boot course or a flat down-the-line kick-out. We are going to attack the guard.

Here is the coaching point: Most defensive ends take a piece of the down blocker and see the guard pulling on the trap. They want to go to the inside and, BOOM! They say they took out the trap man. "I did my job." That is not good enough at Ohio State. You must do more at Ohio State. You don't just go underneath the block. If you coach just that technique you should know that the ball carrier has a downhill running lane. What is the philosophy? Squeeze the attack and make the ball go east and west. This is what we want the end to do against the pulling guard. We want to wrong-arm and pry the man. It is just like the old can opener. You lift and pry. The rule is this: when you wrong-arm and pry you must take out two people. If you do not take out two people, you are not doing the job.

We want to get position on the guard and align with his ear hole and knock him up the field. Why? One of the biggest plays you see is the

Counter Play. They may pull the backside guard and tackle. They may use the backside guard and fullback to block on the play. You want to make sure you make the ball go east and west. We do not want to just take out the lead blocker. We want to take out two people on the play. One of them may be the ball carrier.

On the other side you may get the fullback and I-back coming at the Leo. As Leo comes off the hip of the blocker and sees the fullback starting to attack, he is the first man we see. We go up between the fullback, heavy. We go into him with the inside arm to the fullback. We use the same technique as we use on the pulling guard. We want to take out two men on the play. You really screw the ball carrier up there because he cannot go inside. He is coached to go outside on that play, and there you are. That forces the ball east and west. With our two linebackers scrapping, we tackle the back for a loss. This is how we play the Down Block.

Let's go to the Reach Block. Now the blocker tries to reach block the end. One of the things about the Four-Man Front that is different than Five-Man Front is this: On the Five-Man Front against the Toss Sweep you always wanted to keep your outside arm free. I think you have to do the same thing in most situations today. This is especially true in high school football. As a high school coach I always had this philosophy. There were two ways you were not going to beat me in high school. You were not going to run the Toss Sweep or Option down the field on me, and you were not going to throw the ball over my head. You would have to pound the ball inside all day long to beat me in high school. We did not want them to make the big play on us.

When you play the 4-3, because you are a man short on the front, the linebackers are there to help you out when the ball goes wide. What the line has to be more concerned about is getting off on the ball, attacking and creating a new line of scrimmage. If the ball is outside it is no big deal as long as it is going east and west. I am not saying that we want to get reached. We never want to get reached. The first thing you want to do to the tight end, if he is trying to reach you, is to knock him upfield. I want to keep my feet moving, and I want to lock the blocker out. The key is attacking when the ball is snapped. The ideal way to play the Toss Sweep is to knock the offensive end 2 yards deep on the snap of the ball. That is the key on the Reach Block.

The Over-Reach Block is the move by the blocker to get outside. Instead of taking a short jab step they take a big lateral step and then cross over. They try to get to your inside number. They throw their hip into the block and try to hook you, and they actually hold you. They do this all along the line of scrimmage. Because of this Zone Blocking scheme, the One-Back Offense is very successful. It is because of this scheme. Teams will even get back off the ball on the Zone Scheme. They get as far back off the ball as they can so there is no way you can get into them to attack them.

The way we take care of the Over-Reach is this: We are going to square up a little, and loosen up a little. On the snap of the ball, when the blocker tries to reach me, I attack up, and end up in the same situation as I do on the Reach Block. We drop our inside hand to the blocker's hip and push him upfield. We are coming off low and hard and attacking. We drop that inside hand and push the man upfield.

The next block is the Pass Block. I want to talk about the little things we feel are important on the pass block. When it is first and 10, or second and 4, we are thinking of run. Teams will also show pass on these downs. There are a couple of different ways you are going to see the pass. You will see the Three-Step Pass. This is where the offense will fire straight out and try to hammer you. Also, you will see the offense step back off the ball. First, against the Three-Step, as soon as you take that first step and the offensive man steps out to jab you, we want to throw our hands up. Our ends will swat the ball a lot on the Three-Step Pass.

If the offense goes with the basic Five- or Seven-Step Drop, when the line comes off the ball, we have one key coaching point: When the blocker sets back off the ball, we immediately get to the edge and pass rush. Physically, we are not a good match against the big offensive linemen. We are going to attack one half of the blocker's body; now we have an advantage and have a chance to win.

Next is the Draw Block. There are several ways to run the Draw. The teams that run the Draw the most effective against us are the teams that set up like the pass and then run the Draw. We do not see that very often. Most of the time when offensive linemen are going to run the Draw they are going to open up, but they are going to keep their inside foot on the line of scrimmage. They want to take their hands and knock you upfield and then go out to block the linebacker. If it is a running situation, say a 50-50 run or pass situation, we want to keep it in a run technique. We want to squeeze the blocker and then retrace, and come back down the line and make the play. We want to try to strip the ball.

Next is the Screen Block. We see three types of blocks against the Screen Pass. The offensive linemen will just drop back deep and try to pull you down. That is one technique. Another block is where they drop back off the line of scrimmage and try to cut you down. The other technique is when they drop back and try to knock you upfield and set the Draw a little deeper. We are not really expected to make the play on the Screen Pass. We have to do either one or two things. If we can react quickly enough by reading the offensive back, then we can react. They come way off the line and try to pull you down. There will be a back across your face if it is going to be a Screen. We will react to that type of play. If the back releases inside, we can read it quickly enough and play it down the line. If we are past the back and recognize the Screen late, and we are going after the quarterback, we keep going after the quarterback. Our linebackers are keying those plays and, hopefully, we will force the quarterback to throw the ball into a lot of traffic.

Finishing up on the Run, let's talk about Movement vs. the Run. We have three basic movements we use against the Run. We use the Echo/Lance. They are the same except Echo means End and Lance means Leo. They are the same technique; one to the tight-end side and one to the split-end side. We also use a Slant Technique and a Loop Technique. When do you use movement if you want to stop a run? The basic philosophy is this: First, we use it as a change-up instead of playing Base Technique. It is just a change-up. Second, if we get a big gap we use movement. We may take a defender and just line him up in the gap. If you do not do that, the offense will split you out all day. The third thing we have to do is to bump the linebacker out into coverage. If they come out in an A Set or motion someone to an A Set, we adjust with the secondary and we may have to bump a linebacker out in the coverage.

What do we do on these movements? First, on the Echo and Lance, here are some coaching points. First of all, anytime your ends are moving, you square up your stance slightly. There is no way the end can take a good inside step out of the elongated step. So we will square our stance slightly. We do not square up enough that will allow the offensive man to read it. The second thing we are going to do is to back off the ball a couple of inches. This is where most people make their big mistake. When they go to slant inside, they cheat inside. That is the worst thing you can do. That gives your move away. They know right now if you are going inside. The key is this: Don't cheat inside; just back up a little and square up slightly. That gives you room to clear.

The next coaching point is a short jab step with the inside foot followed by penetrating up in the gap. We do not allow our ends to even look for the football until they have made that full move. Then they can find the football. We do not find the football until we get to the hip of the blocker. We want to make our penetration first. If you do not do that, they will short-step you and you will end up a gap short.

Next we want to key the inside offensive linemen and then react. If you are moving inside, your action no longer is on the man you lined up on. What is great about teaching this position is that everything is the same. If the blocker base blocks me, I will squeeze it back in the gap. If he blocks down, we come running off his hip. If he sets and shows pass, I will get over his outside shoulder and rush the quarterback. Everything is the same for us as a base technique. That is why it is so simple.

The other thing we do on the inside movement is to key the ball as compared to the man over us. We do not care what that man is doing. That is the Echo and the Lance.

Next is the Slant Technique. A lot of the things are the same as on the Echo and Lance. We use this in two basic situations. First, if it is short yardage and we expect a Trap or Dive. The other way is if we have linebackers coming up on the outside. Now we are really concentrating on squeezing the inside gap. We square up slightly and come off the ball a little. Now we step at the inside man's near hip. Now we are attacking the hip instead of going up through the gap. We tell the end if he has to get his helmet and face guard through that man's hip to knock him inside all the way to the center's hip, to do it. If the blocker is turning out and we have our end slanting down, we expect our end to end up on top of the pile. Our whole purpose on the Slant is to restrict everything inside.

The next technique is the Loop. We use the Loop when we expect a team to run a Play-Action Pass, or Bootleg in a normal situation, and we go by tendencies. We line up as we do in Base except we square up a little so the offense can't detect it. Now, we want the end to step four to six inches laterally with the outside foot, followed by an upfield crossover step. You want to get to the hip of the blocker and then you are reacting. It is the same as the inside step, except now we are stepping outside. This is how we work the drill. We have an old-fashioned cage. When we are working on movement by the end we start him under the cage in practice. They have to go inside or outside. If they raise up, they hit their helmet on the cage. If you do not do that in practice, then in a game they will take one step and try to find the ball. Don't let them find the ball until they have completed the technique. On the crossover the arm and leg always come together.

Now we are going to look at Defensive End Play vs. the Pass. Now it is third and long and we expect the offense to throw the ball. Now our mind-set changes a little. One thing is still the same. We are still going to attack. The second thing is that we are going to rush the quarterback. We may not get to the quarterback, but we can get close enough so the quarterback has to get rid of the ball before he wants to. The next thing is to react as you are rushing the quarterback.

Let me go to the Rush Technique. We work on Stance and Alignment. We want to Get Off or Key the Ball. Also we work on our Reactions against all of the same blocks. Here is the difference. First of all, we are in a three-point sprinter's stance. Now that elongated stance is even more elongated. We are in a narrow stance. We align four to six inches outside the blocker's outside foot. Understand one thing: if it is a definite passing situation, that man across from you will be blocking you. We really are aiming at the outside hip of the offensive tackle. We will screw around with the tight end. Sometimes we will line up inside the tight end, sometimes head up with the tight end. The offense does not know where we will line up. This will screw up the tight end's release. We do not want to go into a game and let the offense know where we are going to line up on their tight end.

At the same time, if we know it is a passing situation, we will take our end and line him up and make sure his aiming point is the outside hip of the tackle. It is a race to that point. Everything in practice is set up so we can get to the area beyond the blocker's hip. It is the same principle where we want our whole body on half of his body. It is a race to get to the spot behind the line of scrimmage. Those big offensive linemen have a hard time getting back there. That is one reason the offense likes to go from a Two-Point Stance so they can put the outside leg back. It is a passing situation and we have a Rush Call on. We are keying the ball so we can get off in time.

I will go through the reactions against the different blocks very quickly because we have covered these before. If they come out and try to Base or Reach Block us or to attack us, and it is a passing situation, the only difference is that we are squeezing with a hard outside arm conscious attitude. If they Down Block on us, and we are lined up four to six inches outside the tackle, we are not going to touch him. If he Down Blocks inside and we come across and upfield, and here comes the Sprint Draw, we will see it as we get to the hip of the offensive man. We turn and attack and squeeze it to the inside. Our secondary players are thinking pass and they are back deep. We want to force the ball back inside.

The Reach and Over-Reach Blocks are the same as before. We are a little more outside conscious now. When we have the man locked up we will be skating a little more along the line of scrimmage.

What happens when that man shows pass? We are going to get to the outside edge and use a pass rush technique.

If it is a Draw we are going to retrace and come right back down the original line that I started on (demonstration). We use the Chop on the outside hand. If the blocker has his hands low, we use the Swim Technique. You can't do a Swim Technique if your hips are square. We want to slap and Boom!, we slide the hips. Now we are going to slap the man's butt as we come through to rush the quarterback. If his hands are high, we can use the old Rip Technique. We Rip underneath the man's hands. If we are really good with our hands we may use the karate chop with both hands. If the offense wants to set back and use both hands we can come in and cross our inside hand and put our outside hand over the top of the inside hand in a chopping motion to knock the blocker's hands down when he goes to grab us. That is how we play the pass. We want to get our whole body on one half of the blocker's body and rush the quarterback.

A key coaching point on the Draw: Very rarely does a Draw break straight ahead. Most of the time when a team runs the Draw it starts in the backfield and then breaks to one side or the other. We are going upfield rushing the quarterback and we read Draw. We better not read it too soon. We want to be past the hip of the blocker before we read the Draw. It is a passing situation and I am after the quarterback. I should not be on the line when I read the Draw. I am not going to see the Draw until after I have attacked. When we see it is the Draw, we want to run back down the same line that I started from. I know the ball will break to the spot where I lined up. We do not teach the ends to tackle the man on the Draw. We teach them to strip the ball. The running back does not expect anyone coming back from the outside edge. They are looking for the linebackers. The term we use is to Retrace. We are not satisfied just to make the tackle. We want to cause the fumble.

On the Screen, we react to the type of block the offensive man makes. He is going to try to pull you or he is going to try to cut you or he is going to flash and release. If it is a Passing Situation, you must know what type of Screens the team runs from the scouting report. But the key is the Back. If you get a flare back, a team will use a certain type of Screen Pass and you know what is going to happen.

I want to go over our Pass Rush Stunts. First I will talk about our Two-Man Stunts. We run three Two-Man Stunts. 1) PIC, 2) Pop, and 3) Knife. We all come up with a lot of different terminology in football. Here, in the PIC the "I" means we are trying to free the Inside Man. We are not saying the other man is not supposed to make the tackle. We want to do something special to free up the inside man. PIC means it is just a one-side stunt. When we call Double PIC it means we are stunting on both sides. The PIC means we want to free up the Nose and the End. The Nose and End are always together, and the Tackle and Leo are always together. The End pulls the offensive tackle. The Noseguard steps and flashes his hands at the offensive guard. Then he reaches the outside hip of our end and comes around.

Let me go over both of those techniques real quick. If I am the End and it is a Passing Situation, we are four to six inches outside the tackle. I want to try to free up my buddy to the inside. On my first step, I step at the tackle and pull his outside shoulders inside. I will not release the tackle until I get his outside shoulder perpendicular to the line of scrimmage. At that point, the tackle has had enough time to come around the end. Now the end must release and Rip or Swim and become the inside rusher. We do not want to get knocked past the ball. We want to stay in the pass rush lane where the Noseguard started.

What does the inside man do? He is going to cheat a little inside to the A Gap. We step at the Guard and he sets up for the pass block. The Nose flashes his hands and takes an outside step and reaches for the outside hip of the defensive end. That forces him to make a move upfield. It is not a lateral step, it is up the field. We step, reach, and come so tight off the tail of the end, the quarterback will not see me as I come around. We are only going to pull the tackle if they are Zone Pass Blocking. There is no reason to pull him if they are Man Blocking. If they are in Man, the end comes down inside on the guard and knocks him inside. The tackle will try to pick up the end, and the nose becomes free. If they are Man Protecting, we do not pull anyone; we just run to the inside man.

PIC

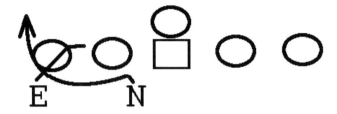

On the POP we do just the opposite. Now the Noseguard is going to pull the guard. We are going to free the OUTSIDE MAN.

POP

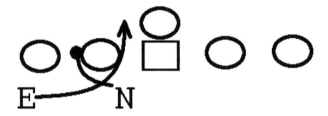

The End is going to step upfield and flash up and come off the butt of the Noseguard. Understand something when you are rushing the quarterback: You have four men rushing, two on each side of the ball. If we have someone on the front four who is not a good pass rusher we take them out of the game at that point.

In practice we move the four down linemen around and let them work from each position. They are basically the same anyway.

Next is the Knife Stunt. It is a little different. The End is lined up six to eight inches outside. That forces the tackle to really widen as he tries to get to the End. That is what we want. As soon as the tackle's shoulders go parallel, the End goes under him. There is no way a 330-pound tackle can get his feet going back to the inside once he starts outside on the block. If we start upfield and the tackle does not open his shoulders to the outside, the end can beat him with speed to the quarterback. The End can't be wrong. The call that is made between the End and Noseguard is a Read Call. The Nose is waiting to see what the End is going to do. He will power rush the offensive guard. He wants to get him coming off the line of scrimmage and get him squared up. He is not going to get his body into the blocker; he rushes with his hands. As the Nose sees the End come inside — BOOM! the Nose goes outside. It's an upfield PIC.

KNIFE

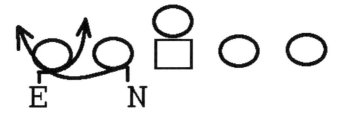

When does the End not come under the tackle? He will not come under if the tackle does not open his shoulders outside, or if the quarterback sprints away. We do not want the Nose coming outside if the quarterback goes the other way. It is a timing thing and it takes practice and practice. The Nose knows if the End has not made his inside move within a two count; he just keeps rushing.

Next we will look at our Four-Man Stunts. All we do is to Double things up. We have a Double PIC, Double Pop, and Double Knife. Both sides are doing the same stunts.

Now we have three special stunts. First is the Flame. We are running a PIC to the Field, and a Pop to the Boundary. We run two different stunts, one on each side. The man to the field side must be a good contain man.

Second, is the Tango. It is a Three-Man Stunt. We use this against a Straight Drop-Back Passing team. We do not expect any type of Sprint-Out. We know the quarterback is going to Drop Back. Now we do an automatic Knife Stunt. We must commit to the inside move. If the blocker's shoulders are square, we grab them and turn the man inside. The Tackle goes inside, the Noseguard flashes, then comes around for the contain. The End has an option. He can straight rush the play, or he can Knife the play. We call this stunt into the boundary because we do not worry about containment on the Drop-Back quarterback into the boundary. Leo is the contain on the Field side of the formation.

The last stunt is Toledo. Teams like to area block inside with the guards and center and Man block with the two tackles. Usually they have two good blocking tackles when they use this scheme. They area block inside because the defense runs twist stunts inside. They lock the tackles on the outside rushers. Toledo screws the offense up. We give quick Knifes to the outside. Now, this forces the offensive tackles to go inside. The inside blockers are sitting inside waiting to see who is going to come to them. All of a sudden the Noseguard comes around the End on the Knife. Now the two guards run into the offensive tackles coming inside on the outside rushers. The Tackle is the contain man on one side, and the Noseguard is the contain man on the other side.

Chapter 3

DEFENSIVE GAP CONCEPTS

Mike DuBose
University of Alabama
1998

Before I get into talking about the actual techniques of playing defensive line, I want to talk a little on our philosophy. This will help you understand what we are trying to get accomplished.

When I left Tampa Bay in 1990 and went back to Alabama as a defensive line coach, our philosophy has stayed primarily the same. We don't have any secrets. Our philosophy has been very simple. We want to prevent our opponent from moving the football with any type of consistency. To do that we have to stop the run. We want to force our opponent into a throwing situation. Once we do that we have to defend the receivers and pressure the quarterback with our front people.

If a team can run the football, it can throw it when it wants to. Therefore it becomes a guessing game. I don't know a defensive coordinator in America—high school, college, or professional—who doesn't like to put the opponent in a situation where it has to throw the ball. When we know they have to throw, we can get our best pass rushers and cover guys in the game.

The second part of our philosophy is our system of defense. That is a little more complicated. When you understand our system, you will better understand what we are trying to do technique-wise. Our system of defense is based on the principle that "You Win Football Games with Football Players who Can Play." You don't win them with coaches and schemes. You can lose football games with coaches. Your players have to believe in the things you believe in. Your defense has to give every kid a chance to make the play on every single play. We don't expect that to happen, but we want our players to believe that. If they feel like they have a chance to make that play, they work harder.

When I first started the coaching defensive line I didn't know anything about it. I sat down and started to study. The one thing I kept hearing everybody say was, "The defensive linemen have to keep the offensive linemen off the linebackers so they can make plays." That is a great system for the linebackers. It is not so good for the defensive line. When we put our guys on the field we want every one of them to feel like they can make a play. The way we play certain blocks in actuality will keep linemen off the linebackers, but we don't ever tell them that. If all he thinks he has to do is keep the linemen off the linebackers that is all he will do. If the ball comes to him he won't make the tackle if he doesn't think that is his job. We tell him to play blockers a certain way, but we never tell him to keep blockers off the linebackers. We want all our people to make that tackle.

We have a philosophy statement: "Don't expect more out of your teammates than you expect out of yourself." Don't expect your teammate to make the play if you're not willing to step forward and make the play.

The second thing we believe in is "Multiple in Alignment Defense." We are the most multiple-front football team in the SEC. We may be the most multiple football team in the country. You need a multiple alignment so you can take advantage of numerous situations. By being multiple, we can take advantage of down and distance, hash marks, line splits, defensive personnel as it relates to the offensive personnel, and hide weaknesses in defensive personnel.

We want a system that is multiple, but is "Not Multiple in Technique." That is very important to us. You develop technique on the field through repetition. I can teach alignment in a classroom. We can have a walk-through and teach alignment. Techniques have to be taught on the field in game-type situations at game-type speed. It has to be full speed, because that is where the reaction is. We can put a defensive lineman head up a center, guard, tackle, or tight end. We can put him on an inside shade on a center, guard, tackle, or tight end. We can put him in an outside shade on a center, guard, tackle, or tight end and only teach him two techniques. We teach him odd or even techniques. We refer to 0, 2, 4, 6, or 8 as even alignments. That is what we got away from but are going back to this spring.

The two-gap philosophy is what we are going back to. When we say two gap, we have two definitions. The NFL has big defensive tackles whom they ask to take on the offensive blocker and cover two gaps. We can't do that. When we get in an even alignment we are a two-gap team before the snap of the ball. Once the play starts we become a one-gap football team. If we have a man aligned in a 4 technique he could have the B or C gap, but not both of them. If we get in an even alignment as a defense, we look like a slant defense because of the keys we are reading.

We line up in "Cheat Alignments." That means as the lineman takes his presnap read, he could be in a 4 Eye Technique if he sees one thing and a 5 technique if he sees something else. It is a read-and-react system. If we are in an odd alignment it is just the opposite. We want to attack the line of scrimmage. We want to get up the field. If we align in a shade on the center, 1 or 3 technique on the guard, 4 eye or 5 technique on the tackle, 7 or 9 technique on the tight end, we want to attack the line of scrimmage. On their step and move-ment they are trying to get upfield. The first step is based upon the pressure point. If the pressure point tells him run, he drives his foot down and gets back into a read technique again. If the pressure point tells him pass, he gets an elongated step.

We want a system that is built around a "Gap Control Principle." We want to be strong in the middle and force the football to the side-lines. The shortest distance to the goal line is a straight line and that is up the middle. The thing that we like is called a "Fit System." That means if the linebacker is in a 4 technique with a defensive end to his outside and a 3 technique defensive tackle, on flow his way, his first step is toward the hip of the defensive end. If flow goes away he flows at the hip of the defensive tackle. That allows the defensive tackle to play aggressive. If he gets reached, the linebacker sees the hip disappear and flows over the top to fit outside. If the tackle gets upfield, the linebacker fits inside him. The linebacker can be more aggressive because the free safety behind him is going to do the same thing.

We want to make sure our defense is well coordinated among our ends, linebackers, and secondary players. If we are playing an option, we want to have someone on the dive, quarterback, and pitch. If it is not an option team, we want someone to contain the end run, some-body responsible for the alley, and someone to take the cut back.

We are going to call about 75 percent of our huddle calls in the two-gap defense. But we are going to play about 80 percent of the snaps in a one-gap principle. We want to make sure we have all 11 people going in the same direction. We are playing what everyone is playing these days. We are playing an attack 4-3 defense. If the ball is working left we want all our defense working that way. The two-gap principle allows that. We get our defensive linemen in pursuit of the ball with their bodies between the blocker and the ball.

We will very seldom play a true two-gap defense. We are going to get out of the two gap into the one gap based upon tendencies, formations, and rush lanes. If we are in a 3-4 package, the outside linebacker is the only one with a defined rush lane. The other three linemen are on tendencies, formations, or rush lanes. The defensive linemen read offensive linemen 90 percent of the time. If a team comes out in an I-formation, we don't see anybody in college that runs the football outside the tackles to the open-end side of the I-formation. That allows us to fire gaps to the tight end. We don't need anybody in the D gap to the open side. We get out of the two gap and into the one gap based upon what the offense tells us at the line of scrimmage.

Let's get into defensive line play. Everything starts with the stance. I've coached the defensive line at all three levels and I don't know that much about it. I'll tell you that right up front. I've tried everything in America. But when you see us, we have the worst stances of anyone you will ever see. What I finally figured out is that everyone is different in his body makeup. A good football position and a stance is one in the same. In a good football position the feet should be slightly wider than the shoulders. The toes should be straight down the field or slightly inside. They are never out. We want a balanced stance with the shoulder, knees, and balls of his feet in line. If they are not, your players are overextended or back in their stance. We teach right- and left-handed stances. If he is on the right side, we want him in a left-handed stance and just the opposite on the left side. From this stance we have to go up the field, right or left, without taking a false step. The first step is always a positive step. It doesn't make any difference where he is going; I want him to gain ground.

You will get tired of hearing me say this but it is one of our fundamentals. One of the most important things is a "Presnap Key." Defenses do the same thing that offenses do. There is not a defensive team in the country that doesn't tell you something they are going to do before you snap the ball. That is doubly true of offensive football teams. If they are going to tell you, you might as well take advantage of it. It is like taking an open-book test and never opening the book until after the test. The information is there, it is just a matter of using the eyes to read it. There are keys in the stance, split, and backfield set. Those are just a few of the things we key.

The next thing I have taught at all three levels. When we are in a cheat alignment, the key is the linemen we line up on and any uncovered linemen either inside or outside him. If we have a nose tackle in a 0 technique with both guards uncovered, the nose tackle keys both guards and the center. The guards will tell him something quicker than the center. The same is true of a defensive end in a 4-eye technique. His key is the tackle he is aligned on and the uncovered guard to his inside. The guard will tell him something quicker than the tackle. That is always the case with our defensive end unless we play a team that is an option team. The quarterback can become an extra blocker by reading the veer. We will single read that type of play. If the ball is going outside, the tackle will zone step and the guard will pull.

If we are in an odd alignment we key the guys we are aligned on. If we came out of the huddle in a third-and-nine play, we would be thinking pass. If the offense came to the line with big splits and rocked in their stance, we would make an "Army" call. That puts us into a different thought pattern. We are now thinking draw. If we give a "Jet" call we key the football to the pressure point. Some guys can't go from ball to pressure point because it happens too fast. If that is the case we go to the pressure point as the key.

We emphasize the hands instead of the flipper and shoulder. That is important to us. When we have our summer camp, most of the kids want to use the flipper. That's fine if that is what you believe in. I believe you have to be stronger to play with the flipper and shoulder, than you do with the hands. The guy that gets his hands inside first usually wins the battle.

The biggest problem you have with defensive linemen is getting them to stay behind their pads and play low. That means playing with his pads down rather then standing up and trying to find the ball. When our freshmen come in I stand in front of them. If their feet are up under them and they are down, the weight has to be on the heels. If he has his feet under him the only place he can go is straight up. We want them to line up with the feet behind the knees.

The second thing is something you need to think about before you say anything. We do not roll the hips when playing blockers. There are only two times we let our defensive linemen roll their hips. One is when they tackle, and the other is rushing the passer. If the lineman rolls his hips there is nowhere he can go but up. It is physically impossible to do anything else. The offensive linemen are taught to hit and roll the hips. If the defense does that, they are helping the offensive blocker. We want to play with our hands and have our feet and hips behind our pads. If the defense is creating the proper angle and leverage point they will win every time.

For the defensive player to be successful there is a progression he has to go through. These three things are sight, defensive reaction or movement, and contact. When you get that progression screwed up the defense is not going to be successful. I don't care what system you teach, what alignment you're in, or what technique you're teaching, it all has to start with sight. He has to see something. The sooner he sees it the quicker he can react to it. If he reacts to it properly than the third phase, contact, becomes the most important phase. Most of the time when you put your linemen in a contact drill, they want to do the third phase first. When we practice, our practice is based on that progression.

The most important item in defensive line play is based on sight. The quicker they can see it the quicker they can react to it. That goes for linebackers and defensive backs, also. Every drill we do we stress the eyes. Defensive linemen are always in a contact situation in what we call a "contact zone." When he picks his foot up he has to get it down quickly. There is nobody on the football field who has to make a decision more quickly than a defensive lineman. No one lines up as close to the ball as he does.

We don't ever want to be guilty of underestimating our players. I never tell our players they can't do something. I never want to hear one of our coaches say that. That is the worst thing he can do. It is only when we ask too much of our players that we can find out what real ability they have.

The last thing is, "We are going to be physical." That is one thing I demand. We are going to be known as the most physical team you will face.

Here is a coaching point about tackling: We never ask our defensive linemen to put their face mask on the numbers in tackling. We want them to step on the back's toes and tackle with their chests. Our linemen are all about 6'5". If they start putting their face mask on a 5'11" back, they are going to be overextended and off balance.

Let me spend some time talking about pass rushing. When we rush the passer, we want to run as straight a line as we can to the passer. We also want to make the offensive linemen move their feet. If a back tries to run over a defender, will he make the tackle? It may not be pretty but he will make the tackle. If the back puts on a move, it makes it harder for that defender to make the tackle. That is the same idea in pass rushing. We don't want to run right down the middle of the offensive linemen. The average five-step drop pass is thrown in 2.8 to 3.2 seconds. If I run over the offensive lineman, the throw will come off. We want to make him be an athlete. The key to rushing the passer is to get an arm and hip through or past the offensive lineman's hip. If you are rushing on the right side of the lineman, the key is to get the left hip through to that side. It doesn't matter if you use a rip, swim, or some other move. The rush is a game of angles. Once we get the hip through, we get back on the straight line to the quarterback. The rusher wants to keep his hips, shoulders, and feet square to the quarterback.

We give our pass rushers a two-way go. We base that off the pressure point of the offensive blocker. The aiming point of the rush is an imaginary shoulder wider than the pressure point. It is at the outside shoulder if he is rushing outside and at the inside shoulder if he is rushing inside. That forces the offensive blocker to move his feet. If you have an athletic quarterback who likes to run out of the pocket, you may not want your containment rushing inside. In that case we may give him only an outside rush.

If the pressure point jumps outside on the rusher, he directs inside. If the pressure point doesn't change, he continues to rush outside. If the pressure point doesn't move inside or outside, but back, that is when we power rush over the lineman. He has set his weight back and can't stop the defensive end's momentum.

When the pass rusher starts to rush the passer, he should already have a pass-rush technique in mind and a counter move off it. The only thing that is predetermined is pressure point and aiming. The other moves come from sight, reaction, and contact. The pass-rush move is based on the height of the shoulders. If the shoulders are up, the pass rusher is going to rip through. If the shoulders are down and forward, we are going to swim.

Here is the actual technique. The offensive lineman's shoulders are up. For a rusher coming off the left side, he is going to rip with the right arm. He tries to set it as deep under the arm of the offensive tackle as he can get it. His left foot has to widen so his right foot can clear the hip of the blocker. The right arm rips up and under the right arm of the blocker. After the hip comes through, the rusher takes his left hand and throws it toward the quarterback. That actually pulls the blocker's shoulder around so he ends up on the rusher's back. The offensive blocker is actually pushing the rusher toward the quarterback.

If the rip occurs and the hip doesn't get through, the rusher pivots like a basketball player and spins back to the inside to the quarterback. We never spin if the hips are through unless the quarterback steps up inside the pocket. In that case he might spin and try to get back inside. We don't predetermine the spin. It is a counter move to be used if the hips don't get through.

If the offensive linemen has his weight back, the rusher wants to power rush. The only option for the lineman to stop the power rush is to stop his feet and lock out. That gets him overextended. The rusher goes back to the swim move and goes right by him.

We play some offensive blockers that are extremely aggressive. On the first rush we want to power rush him. We want him to get over-aggressive. That makes it easier to use moves on him later in the game.

When we run our two-man stunts, we never call them in the huddle. It is always called at the line of scrimmage. If we have a tackle-tackle stunt between a 3 technique and a shade technique, we know the 3 technique is going to be the penetrator. He is coming inside and trying to get penetration on the center. He is trying to get hip-to-hip penetration on the center. The shade tackle is coming around. The guard has a decision to make. If he stays with the 3 technique tackle, the shade tackle comes free. If he comes off for the shade tackle, the 3 technique tackle has the center pinned and can make the play.

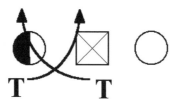

The only way the defense can win is if the offense doesn't stop the penetrator. From the tight 3 technique, the tackle makes a move upfield and dives hard inside to beat the center.

Chapter 4

DEFENSIVE DRILLS

Mark Duffner
University of Maryland
1995

What I'm going to talk about is defense and defensive drills. I'm going to give you every drill we use. I think the little things make a difference in the success you have as a football team. It helps in particular on defense.

We talk a lot about techniques and fundamentals at our place. One of the first things is fumble recovery. That goes for our entire football team, not just the defense. They need to know how to properly cover a football, how to cradle it, and when to Scoop and Score. It is amazing how many kids on our team don't know how to recover a football. We work real hard to make our kids understand that if they can't advance the ball they should cradle it. So many kids have the ball up in the chest or lay on top of it. I think it is important in drills that you teach them how to cradle the ball or scoop it and score with it. Their eyes and hands have to come down to the ball. They have to pick up the ball and put it away before they start to run.

I going to talk a lot about tackling. It doesn't matter whether you are a 4-4, 4-3, or 5-2 defense. If you don't tackle well, you are not going to be a good team.

We are big on enthusiasm. I think it is important to have proper celebration of big plays. If a young man makes a big play on the football field, we'll say, "Give 'em Three." Our kids, on the count, will clap three times. I'll say, "Give 'em Three; one, two, three." The kids will give three rapid claps. It is a simple little thing, but everybody likes to be recognized. When we make big plays on offense or defense we do not try to taunt. But we like to get together and have some fun with that. We practice High Fives. When we got to Maryland, the previous

35

coaches had not done that type of stuff. They thought we were really out to lunch. We blow a double horn in practice and practice High Fives. We have the greatest High Fives in the country. I promise you that. I think it is important to coach enthusiasm and that is just one way we do it.

Coach Fran Ganter talked last night about ball security. He used the words "Overprotect the football." We call it "Iso the Ball." That is like Isokinetics the football against the rib cage. We teach our entire team what that is all about. We don't want to get careless with the ball. We do the ball-wrestling drills, and we probably picked them up from Penn State. Those are excellent drills you can do in the off-season for ball security. We talk to our players about the football and how important it is to the game. The game cannot be played without the ball. The defense is trying to get the ball and the offense is trying to keep it. There is 13 pounds of air pressure in the football. We talk about it being gold. We talk about protecting those "13 pounds of gold." We have to protect the football at all times.

We teach our kids how to Iso the ball, and we teach them how to strip the ball. We teach them how to properly strip the ball. Kids don't know how to do it. If you can pull the running back's wing up from his body, that exposes the ball. We can punch or pull the ball out.

We teach ball skills to everyone on the team.

1) We teach these drills to everyone. It is important to everyone on the team to understand how to catch the ball and secure it.

2) We use a tennis ball a lot to improve our hand strength. They can sit at home watching TV and squeeze the ball. That strengthens the grasp in catching the ball and tackling.

3) Some of our coaches can't throw the ball very far. If you are coaching the secondary, in order to practice a deep-ball drill, you have to throw the ball deep. We use a youth football. It is smaller and it is amazing how far you can throw that thing.

4) We use the "Ball on a String." That is a whiffle football on an elastic strap. It has a hook on the end so you can attach it to a fence. You throw the ball and it comes back. You can work on your hand and eye coordination in catching the ball. We use this during preseason camp and all through spring practice. You can get 25-50 catches in a couple of minutes. The focus is on catching.

5) We use softballs in our program to teach eye and hand coordination. We have two guys across from each other. One man rolls the ball to the other man to his right and then to his left. This is the drill that lots of baseball teams use. All we want them to do is bend their knees and focus on the target. They get in good position with bent knees and focus on the target.

6) We coach catching the ball. We use a drill called making "Two Catches." We want to catch the ball twice. Catch the ball properly with the finger tips and put the ball away. Catch and Iso the ball are the two catch phrases in catching the ball.

Another thing you can do to help with the grasping of the ball is by doing "Towel Pull-Ups." We do a great job with all our weight programs. We do Power Cleans, Bench Presses, Inclines, and Squats. But to improve your hand strength, hang a couple of towels from your chin-up bar. Make your players grasp the towel and do pull-ups.

I want to get into tackling. As we analyze our tackling, here are some of the reason we do poorly:

1) Lost vision of the target. We talk about burning our eyes through the target.

2) Feet stopped. We make contact and our feet do not continue to move through the tackle. We want to hit to and through the man.

3) Too narrow a base.

4) We lunge at the ball carrier instead of proper position.

5) No wrap-up. We haven't locked our arms or grabbed cloth. Those are the most common reason why we miss tackles.

Here are some tackling tips. We talk about playing defense with good power position. It is important to put into your kids' minds what a good football position is. We talk about getting in a bent-knee position. That gets them into good power angles and good position. Enter the contact area in a good power angle position. We want to keep our heads up and eyes open. We want to hit on the rise as we make contact. We want to hit to and through the man. We want to accelerate and widen our feet through the contact.

Let's get into how we actually teach tackling:

1) The first thing we do is to fit them into position. We put our tacklers in a good bent-knee position. We call it "Being in Position to Bite the Football." The coach simply puts them into a position

for a perfect tackle. He grabs cloth in the back so he understands what the perfect position is.

2) The next thing we do is get into the fit position and work on nothing but the arm punch to grab cloth.

3) The third thing we do is to put them into the fit position and work on hip roll. We use no arms. We work on belly bumps, which teaches the hip roll. We don't want to tackle with our legs straight and our hips away from the target. We get into the fit position, hands behind the back, and belly bump.

4) The fourth step is to get into the close fit position and go through the whole technique. We arm punch, hip roll, and use foot acceleration. We are not trying to knock anybody down or hurt anybody. We want them to understand the procedure and steps to tackling.

5) We get one step from contact and do the same thing getting movement backward.

6) Sometimes we do the drill with shields. The runner puts a light bag right on his chest so we can feel the hit through the man.

This drill is called "Finishing the Play." We do our bag drills. As the players come over the last bag I've got a cone there. I can do a number of things. I can put a man there where they would execute a form "Wrap-up Tackle" on the man. They are not taking the man down. There may be a football at the end where they have to scoop it up and score. I am doing my agility drills over the bag and at the end I am teaching them to accelerate toward a target. We want to finish the play.

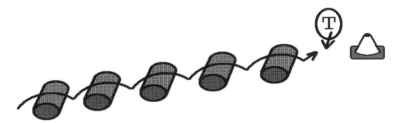

We do the same thing with the sled. We do our hand shivers up and down the sled. At the last dummy, we do the same thing as we did in the bag drill. They accelerate toward the target, wrap-up tackle, or scoop and score with the ball. We coach them to attack downfield and focus on a target.

The next drill deals with leg protection. If your players can't protect their legs they won't get to the tackle area. Linebackers may be big and strong, but if they can't protect their legs they won't be very good. The key words to the drill are "Push and Give a Step." From the bent-knee position we get our hands on the target, push it down, and get our feet back. The eyes and hands go to the target and the feet are kicked back. We teach this at all of our positions. It is like a wrestling move to avoid a takedown. I don't try to step in and deliver a blow because that brings the legs to the target. We push off, give ground, and make a play. We line up three cones from hash marks to sideline. The defender shuffles down on each cone. He pushes, gives ground, and proceeds to the next cone. After the third cone we have the "Finish-The-Play Drill." We have a person or ball where we "Wrap-up Tackle" or scoop and score. You can use heavy bags in the next progression where they actually push on the bags and move their feet away.

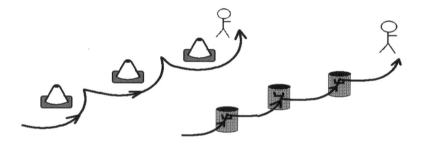

The best part of this drill is when you put people into the drill. Where the bags or cones were, we put three people on all fours. As the defender comes down the line the guys on all four lunge out and try to grab the defender's feet. The coaching point is the defender is not trying to strike a blow. The defender shuffles, pushes, and gives ground as he comes toward the sideline. After the third guy the defender accelerates and finishes the play. The guys on all fours are trying to actually tackle the defender. It is a great drill.

Before you go on the field make sure your players understand what you want them to do. Go over it with them on the board so the drill makes sense to your players.

The next progression is to put guys in a staggered line in a two-point stance. The defender shuffles down gaining ground upfield. As he comes upfield we try to chop him down with a chop block. The defender is taking on the real deal now. That is the progression we do these drills. Once your kids learn the drills, you can rip through them in no time at all. After we have gotten the fundamentals down we progress to the next drill which is harder than the one before. We have never gotten anyone hurt in these drills.

We do a drill we call a "Chop Drill." This is a live drill. We do this for two and a half minutes. If you go five minutes, it gets boring. We divide our team up. We have receivers against the defensive backs, tight ends on the linebackers, and so on. We even the groups out so we don't have a big group at one place and a small group at another. We line our defenders on the 1-yard line and the offense on the next yard line. We mark off about a 5-yard zone in which we run the drill. We place two cones on the yard lines with the defender and offensive man facing each other about 5 yards from the cones in the middle of the lines. The offensive man runs to the cone either way. He runs a track to the cone. The defender shuffles toward the cone. The offense tries to chop the defender. The defender uses his "Push-and-Give Technique." It is very rapid-fire working the best on the best. We set up five stations with our defensive backs, outside linebackers, inside linebackers, defensive line, and ends. You can get a lot of snaps, good toughness for the offense, and good leg protection for the defense on this drill.

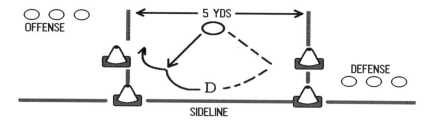

I'm going to show you our tackling stations. We call it our "Tackling Circle." We got this from the Air Force Academy about 10 years ago. We use 50 yards of the football field and set up four stations on that section of field. I'll go through all the stations for you in a minute. We do the tackling circle for 10 minutes. We go two minutes and 15 seconds of repetition at each station. We move clockwise in our station.

There are two things we take advantage of in these drills:

1) We get phenomenal repetition of tackling in a condensed period.

2) We have the same coach at each drill who gets to see the entire defense. He gets a chance to evaluate the entire defense as it comes to his station. After practice in the coaches' meeting, everyone has some input on the defense.

We have four stations. We divide our team up into groups as equal in number as we can. If we have 40 defensive players, we want 10 kids at each station. We go over the drills before we start. You may want to walk through this the first time you do it. We don't want a Chinese fire drill. This is the greatest tackling teacher there is. In preseason camp we had two of these drills going on. I wanted our offensive guys to know how to do this, too. We don't want the drills far apart. We do not want to waste time going from drill to drill. After the horn blows, everyone in the drill comes to the coach, then jogs clockwise to the next drill. When we do the drill the next day, the players start one station ahead of where they started the day before. We don't want them to start each day at the same spot. They will get bored with that.

DRILL 1
SIDELINE TACKLE

DRILL 2
SCORE
TACKLING

SHED TACKLE
DRILL 4

SHOOT
TACKLING
DRILL 3

You can use any drill you want. These are the drills we use. The first drill we use is a "Sideline Tackling Drill." We line up the tackler and the ball carrier 10 yards apart on the hash mark. The ball carrier starts to run about three-quarters speed toward the sideline at an angle. The defender closes from the inside out, and makes a good punch through, wrap-up tackle. We are not taking anyone down, but we are going to thump the ball carrier. The ball carrier runs tall. They change lines and the next guys comes. We don't always have footballs for all the guys. They have to make believe the ball is in the outside arm. The defensive backs do this drill all the time, but how many times do you do it with defensive linemen? They get caught in this technique sometimes in a game. When we get more sophisticated we let the back make one move like a cutback.

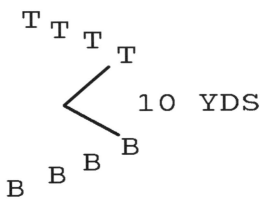

The next station is what we call "Score Tackle." We have defenders about 1 yard from the sideline. We put a bag down in the middle of the 5-yard lines. The defender lines up on the bag which is about 2 yards from the sideline. The ball carrier is on the other side of the bag. The ball carrier runs one side of the bag or the other and tries to score. The score is across the sideline. The defender is trying to hit the ball carrier above the knees, with his head on the outside. He widens the feet and knocks him out of bounds. The out-of-bounds lines are the 5-yard lines. This is not live as taking him to the ground. It is live, knock-the-dog-crap-out-of-someone type of hits.

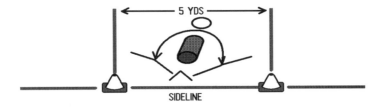

The third station is called "Shoot Tackle." We use bags for this drill. You can use jerseys or towels instead if you choose. We use five bags. This is the old "Eye-Opener Drill." The ball carrier runs down the dummies and picks an alley to run through. The defender shuffles down the other side of the dummies. Once the ball carrier turns up into the lane of dummies the tackler comes into the alley and makes the proper tackle. He uses the techniques I talked about earlier. We are not putting anyone on the ground, but we are thumping them pretty good. The ball carriers stay over on their side the first time through. That way we get to shuffle right and left. After the second time they change sides.

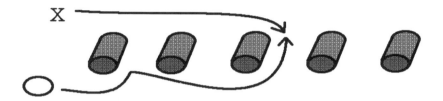

A drill that we use for a change-up is called "Explosion Tackling." This keeps your people from getting bored. Find some tumbling mats. If you can't find some, go to a garage sale and buy some old mattresses. We put the ball carrier a yard from the mat and tackle him onto the mat. That teaches follow-through. In all the other drills we don't take the guy down. On this one we want the guy put on his back. The mat prevents injury. We don't want to hurt people. That is the reason for the mat. The tackler takes one to two steps to make contact.

The next station is our "Shed Tackling Drill." We alter the drill for the position that is participating in the drill. Make the blocks fit the positions you are working with. If it is defensive backs, they generally play chop blocks. If it is a defensive linemen, he sheds a drive block. The tempo is about three-fourths speed. There are two ball carriers. The lineman has to take on the drive block, shed the block, and tackle the ball carrier. He doesn't know who is carrying the ball. The coach points at the ball carrier he wants to carry the ball.

As a change-up drill we use what we call a "Peel Drill." We line up three guys in a staggered line. The defender is 5 yards away from the first guy. The blockers start to move outside. They can block the tackler high or low. The tackler shuffles out, takes on the first blocker, sheds, and takes on the second blockers, sheds, and tackles the last man in the line. They rotate through the drill.

We don't use the circle every day. In preseason we develop two different circuits. We do one in the morning and one in the afternoon. It is important to coach in the shed period. One of the biggest thing in tackling is getting off the block. It is great to have a scheme, but if your players can't get off a block, forget the scheme. We teach the shed like the fit tackling. It is like they have taken on a block and we stopped the camera. We coach bent knees, pad under pad, extend arms, and get rid of the blocker. On the first step there is no resistance from the blocker. The second step there is resistance from the blocker. This is the same idea as the "Fit Tackle."

This next drill you can do in your off-season program. You don't need a ball for this. When you are teaching fundamentals and agility, you can teach tackling in this drill. We set up a square with cones 5 yards apart. We put one cone in the middle. The ball carrier lines up on one corner of the square. He runs to the middle and breaks to either side of the middle cone. The tackler lines up in the opposite corner, mirrors the ball carrier, and makes a good fundamental tackle. Eventually the ball carrier runs toward any cone in the square, the tackler mirrors him and makes the tackle. We are not trying to see who is tough. We are working on fundamentals.

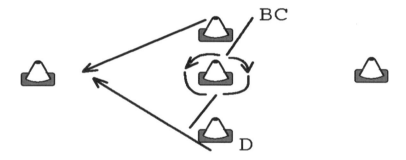

The next drill is like the "Score Drill." We set up the cones 10 yards apart in a square. The ball carrier starts on one corner and runs toward the middle of the square. The tackler starts on the corner opposite the ball carrier on the same side. The ball carrier tries to score. He has a larger area to execute his moves. The tackler takes his inside-out path and makes the tackle. This is a live drill. We are not taking anyone down, but making the big thud hit. You can also do this in a gym, but not in a full contact situation.

The next drill is a "Pass-Rush Drill." The coach stands in the middle of the lined cones, which indicate a pass-rush lane. He calls a cadence but the linemen are reacting to the movement of his foot or a ball. They take off on the movement. They touch the cones, lean against the cone representing the quarterback, and race back to the line. We are coaching takeoff. The cones are set up about 5 yards apart.

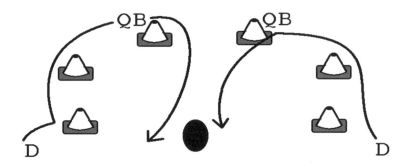

We have a drill we call the "Chase Drill." This is a good Offense vs. Defense drill. We line the drill up between the sidelines and the hash marks. The offensive man gets a spot equal distance between the numbers and the hash. We have two defenders. One man has his toes at the bottom of the numbers and the other man has his toes on the hash. There is a coach on either end of the box. The offensive man runs to one of the coaches. He tries to make the tackler between him and the coach miss. The second tackler is chasing the ball carrier and trying to strip the ball. The ball carrier has 10 yards in which to make his move. The offense can score in either direction. He has to beat one tackler to score. This is a good toughness drill and gives a true picture of what happens in a game. We tell the chase tackler to strip the ball carrier if he is up. He is not to hit him if he is down. If you don't have numbers on your field, the ball carrier takes a position equal distance between the two tacklers.

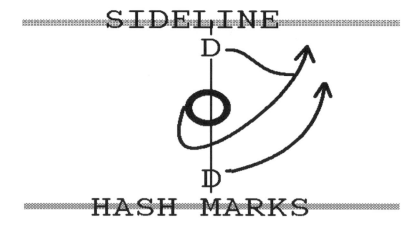

We have a "Special Circuit" we use. This is a spin-off of the Tackling Circuit and it is like the Tackling Circle. We have four drills that everyone goes to. You can use any drills you want. We use Fumble Recovery, Pass Rush, Tackling, and Strip Drill. When you do this you are not leaving it up to chance for the little things that make a great defense.

We went a step further. We went to a "Block Protection Circuit." In those four stations we had Chop Block, Shed, Stalk Block, and High Block Drills. The coaches don't move. They stay in the drill and the defensive players come to them. He coaches the same drill over and over so everyone gets the same teaching. We spend 10 minutes in these circuits and no more. We go two minutes and 10-15 seconds per drill. The defensive line goes through the Stalk Block Drills just like the defensive backs. The defensive backs go through the Shed Drill just like the linemen.

The "Alley Drill" is a terrific drill. What I am showing you is what I show the kids. I recommend you do it, if you use this drill. It keeps the drill from looking like a fire drill. This is a great Shed Drill. It is an emotional and a tackling drill. It is a tough, intense drill. You have to set the drill up properly. We set the stations up between the sideline and 5 yards on the other side of the hash mark. The alley is 10 yards wide. At the ball there are two dummies 5 yards wide. We place shirts at an angle going back to the sideline from the dummies. It looks like a funnel as it goes toward the sideline. The alley starts out 5 yards wide and ends up 10 yards wide. We have an offensive and defensive lineman on the cone 5 yards outside the hash mark. There is a wide receiver on the hash mark. The defensive back is 10 yards off the ball. The ball carrier is 5 yards behind the linemen. We have two one-on-one blocks with the line blocking on the line, and the wide receiver stalking the defensive back. This is a live drill. This is a great drill.

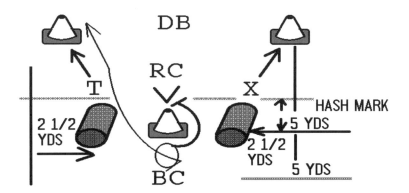

We have several of these stations set up. You have to script who you want going against whom. The coach calls the cadence for the offense.

The "3-on-3 Drill" is similar to the Alley drill. It is a 10 yards-by-10 yards area with three offensive linemen on three defensive linemen. One ball carrier tries to score. The offense has three downs to score. The ball is brought back to the middle each time. This teaches coming off the ball, knocking them back, and to score. This is a high-emotion drill that is completely live. Again you should script who you want going against whom. We don't often put our defensive backs in this drill. There are no reach blocks or trap blocks in the drill. It is straight drive blocking. If the defense can keep the offense from scoring they win. If the offense scores on the first play they come back and run two more. It is a three-play rep.

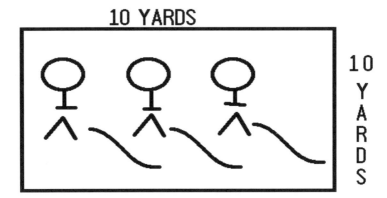

With that drill we do the "Terp Drill." It is the old Oklahoma Drill. It is one-on-one blocking between the bags with a ball carrier. We set up four stations and run them two at a time. We run the 1's and 3's together and the 2's and 4's together. That way we can watch two stations at once. The backs are 5 yards behind the offensive blocker trying to score. The bags are about 3 yards apart. The defensive coaches tighten up the bags and the offensive coaches widen them.

A drill we do with our defensive backs and linebackers is called the "Bounce Drill." The ball is lined up on the hash mark. There are two defensive backs and two wide receivers. The coach tosses the ball to the running back and he tries to get wide. The defensive backs play the stalk blocks of the wideouts and make the tackle. These are high blocks. If you have your defensive backs working in this drill you could even throw the ball. That makes the defensive backs read "On-the-Line and Off-the-Line" action of the quarterback.

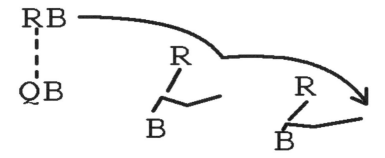

The last thing I want to get to is the "Pursuit Drill." We use the whole field with five cones set up on the sidelines on each side of the field. We have five stand-up dummies for the offensive line spacing. The ball is in the middle of the field. We put two cones 5 yards off the line in the backfield. We line up our defense. This is "Perfect Play" time.

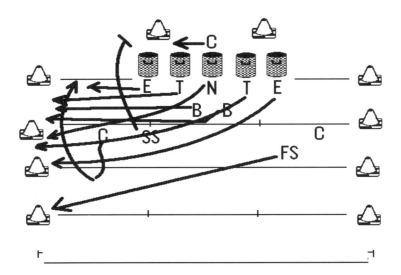

We line up in the techniques and proper stances which go with the defense. The second-team defense is lined up holding those bags. The guys holding the bags move them on cadence. That gives us "Takeoff." The coach gives direction. The corner and safeties are running their Force and Fill angles on the ball. The onside end and tackle, and both inside linebackers are sprinting to the first cone and executing a tackle. The nose guard and backside tackle are running to the second cone. The backside end is running to the third cone, and the backside corner is running to the fourth cone. They are all executing a tackle at the cone.

Chapter 5

DEFENSIVE LINE TECHNIQUES

Bill Glaser
University of Kentucky
1991

I will talk about the Multiple Defense. Everything I am going to show you is how we line up in our positions for our different fronts. We are in multiple fronts so we can give the offense problems. How you play the man off the ball, or the linebacker, is the key. How the linebackers react is the key. The man up front must smash the man up front that is going to block on him. He has to do that and hold the gap. How the linebacker fills the gaps are the keys. The linebacker may have the gap between the guard and tackle, but how he takes that gap is important. Is he going to attack the gap as soon as he sees flow toward that gap? Is he going to spy, or hover, and then when he sees the ball go in the gap, get into the gap? Is he going to line up outside and stunt to that gap regardless of where the ball goes? The man off the ball is the key. This is a key point.

There are some rules you have to learn to play this defense. Coach Larry New (see Chapter 11) talked about our 31 Defense. The first number is for the tackle and the second number is called for the nose. If only one number is called it is for the tackle. The tackle is in a 3 technique and the nose is in a 1 technique. Everyone else is in our base alignment. The Ends' base is a 5 technique. Mike and Will play their 1 and 3 techniques. The rover and bandit go according to the coverage. The strike does have one thing that he has to do here. Any time the strike sees the tackle down inside over the guard, he has to sight adjust in a cinch alignment inside the tight end. If the strike hears the call for the tackle is a 3 or a 1 he knows he must play a cinch technique. He is in the old 7 technique inside the end.

51

I want to go over our gaps. We do not number the gaps. We call our gaps letters. The A gap is between the center and guard, B is between the guard and tackle, C is between the tackle and end, and D is outside the end.

Before Coach Curry came to Kentucky we were a reading defense. Now, in this defense we are a smashing type defense. We must be strong up front in this defense. Our linemen must smash the blocker as they come off the line of scrimmage. It comes down to who is going to block whom. In a sense, we are trying to block the offense. It was a hard adjustment for our linemen this year.

This is what we start off telling our defense people: "No one can make you better than you want to be." We have to motivate these big players to get them to play better. "You can lead a horse to water, but you can't make him drink." But, we do believe we can make him thirsty. Our job as coaches is to lead the players to the water and make them thirsty. I let them know it is up to each player how good he wants to become. If they have the desire and have good size and strength they can become good in this defense.

The key to the defense is sound techniques. This is what we mean by sound techniques:

1. Footwork—We must have sound footwork or it will kill us. A lot of people do not run the film properly to see the footwork. The first thing I grade is the first step. I want to see if he takes the first step properly. If he takes the first step wrong he is beat. That is the only way I know to force them to take the proper first step, and that is why we grade that first step.

2. Body position—This is what we want:
   a. Below pads

   b. Corner of blocker

A good thing about this defense is that we are playing on the corner of people now. If we take the proper steps the offense can't tie us up and get on the corner. We do not want the man to get head up with us because he can hold us from the head-up position. We want to be on the corner of the blocker after we take our first step.

3. Use of hands separation—If you do not block with the hands we are going to kill you. Everyone blocks with his hands.

4. Keep head up—Don't hit with the top of your head. Bring the head up when you make contact.

5. Recognize, React, and Tackle—This comes from reading blocking schemes.

Next is our Basic Principles of Defensive Line Play:

1. Stance—Most of the time we are going to be in a three-point stance. It is tough when the players have to learn the stance from both sides. We may put the other hand down to a four-point stance if they are having problems with the three-point stance.
   a. Go in any direction with ease.
   b. Never tip off our direction.
   c. Step with either foot. Eliminate false steps.

2. Alignment
   a. Lateral—as close to head up as possible (ability).
   b. Vertical—on or back off the line of scrimmage. Depends on how good the man can read. If he can read, he is up on the ball; if he is a slow reader, he is back off the ball. By backing off the ball you do give up a little because the offense can adjust the block.

3. Concentration—They have to concentrate on playing the defensive line. How do you practice this? You have to make practice as rapid-fire as possible. You have to repeat the drills over and over after you have taught them what you want.

To teach all of this to the defensive line we feel you must Chalk It, Talk It, and Walk It. We get so wrapped up with intensity that we forget at times to take them out on the field and walk them through what we want. This is the way to teach football. Then, in the concentration part, you can go out and really put pressure on them to move a lot faster. Teach them first.

STANCE—We are in a three-point stance. We want to be toe to instep, with the weight evenly distributed. I tell them the shade foot is going to be back. That is the foot that I am going to cover the man up with. We want the toes straight ahead. I want a balanced stance. If I get in a three-point stance and put my hand down the middle of my body, it is going to turn my shoulders and I will be cockeyed. The hand should be right out from my big toe. Your weight should be forward on the balls of the feet. The uncovered hand is the hand I have in the gap. I want to get into a position to grab the cuff of the blocker. We stress these points:

STANCE

a. Feet

b. Hands

c. Weight distribution

d. Eyes on blocker

On alignment, the starting point is foot to crotch. We want to hug the ball so the blocker can't knock us off the line. We start out teaching the lineman hugging the ball and let them come off the ball and explode into the blocker. That is how we start them out.

ALIGNMENT

a. Foot to crotch

b. Hug the ball

CONTACT

a. Step with the covered foot

b. Face mask in the "V" of neck

c. Hands - Pec and cuff

d. Smash and strain

With the legal aspects in our times we have to be careful. If we say hit with the hat and head we may get sued. What we tell them is to keep the eyes up and to put the face mask in the "V" of the neck of the blocker. The one hand comes up to the pec and the other hand comes up to the cuff.

We teach this drill from the six-point stance and the three-point stance. We take a lot of reps on the six-point stance. Then we come up to the three-point stance and work on that aspect of the defense.

BLOCK REACTIONS—This is how we teach them to react to the blocks. We are going to teach them to react to the right shade and the left shade. We want them to react to the drives, cutoff, and reach blocks.

A. Drive block—We do not get a log of drive blocks on this defense. But if you can't handle the drive block you will see a lot of it. You better be able to handle the drive block, and you have to teach it first. In our scheme because we stunt so much we do not get much of the drive block unless it is the double time. We still have to play the drive block. If we do get the drive block we step with the shade foot and pec and cuff, and strain inside.

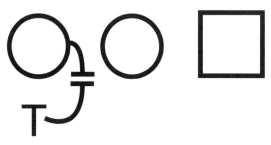

B. Cutoff block—The term cutoff can screw you up. If you have the inside gap and the blocker is trying to keep you out of that gap is it reach or cut off block? As the blocker tries to cut us off from the gap we want to step with the inside foot first and keep the shoulders square. We tell them to throw their butt in the hole. This helps us square back up.

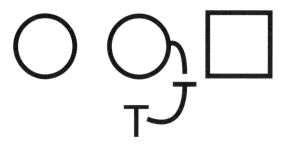

C. Reach block—This is the only time we step with the outside foot first. We want to stay square. I am in a right shade technique. My right shoulder is on his shoulder. My right foot is back. That is my cover foot. My outside arm is free. It is the same if he is lined up on the center or guard or tackle; we are in a right shade.

Next is the cutback play. We play *through* the gap. The cross-face technique gives up the line of scrimmage. That is the worst thing we can do on the play. Don't cross face. We run a mirror drill and go one on one at three-quarter speed. We get all of the line and line them up. We put the offense in their position. I tell them they are going to be in a right shade. They all step to the right of the blockers. Right shade means right foot back, right hand down. I will signal to the offense the type of block that I want the offensive man to simulate. We work on the three blocks as we covered above. We get down and take one step. It is a mirror drill and that is all it is. I will call out, "Set, Go." The defensive man has to react to what he reads. It is just one step. We are working on footwork. We work on the three blocks and we can give them a lot of reads and they can get good at this drill. We flip the offensive people around after we go through all of the blocks. It is a good drill and the players do not mind it at all. After everyone has had a chance on defense we switch back to the first group and work on the left shade. We do the same thing as we did before. This way everyone gets work and everyone can get better. You can work every player, JV and varsity. You never know when you will have to use some of those players. At Kentucky we know we will have to play some of those young players at the end of the season. We coach all of them so they can get ready to play when they are called on.

Now that we have the read down we want to do some stunting. This is how we are going to stunt. We want to attack them. As soon as the ball moves we want to smash the offensive line. If we get into the wrong gap, we still want to smash the blocker. We want to hold that line and create a pile at the line of scrimmage. There are three ways to secure the hole. One, you are in the hole. Two, he is in the hole. Three, I get my head and eyes in the hole. If the back sees the head and eyes in the hole he will not hit in that gap.

Now, we call our 3 Jet. We have a number and a word. Now, we know the number is a read, and the word is a stunt. On the read we went on the movement of the blocker. When we run a stunt we go on the snap of the ball.

STUNT TECHNIQUES

a. Same stance and alignment

b. Hug the ball

c. Go on the snap

d. Exact footwork

e. Eyes on your man - stunt and redirect

We feel we will stunt better if we go on the snap. This is how I think you can improve your defense. If you can get them to go on the read and the snap they will be a lot better. If you will read when you play straight and go on the snap on stunts. If he will go on the snap he will go to where he is supposed to go on the stunt. If we are going outside on a stunt, I want to take the first step with the outside foot. If I am going to stunt inside, I will step with the inside foot first. Don't change their stance, you don't have to. You can do it, but you have to work on this. Again, it comes with concentration. We want to look at the man we are going on.

We have two ways in which we stunt. First, I am going to change gaps. We call it a Fire when we are going to change from a B gap to an A gap on the snap of the ball. How do we do it? We have the same stance and we want to make it look like we are reading. We are in a 3 technique going to a 1 technique. That would be a 31 Fire for us. We key the blocker as we step. If the blocker goes away from the way I am going, I make my step and square up. The blocker will probably go on by me. I do not want to run into the A gap and then try to get out to the B gap. They want you to waste three steps by going down inside the A gap. We step laterally and then take one, two, and I am in the B gap.

This is the tough thing to do. Now, we want to go to the a gap and he is going to try to cut me off through the A gap. As I step laterally I do not have a lot of power. We want to get into the A gap and he is trying to keep us out of the A gap. We put our face in the "V" of the neck and mash him down inside. We block him down inside all the way to the sideline as hard as we can. You will crate a big pile if you will explode on the move to the gap.

This is the total influence we give a blocker. This is the total package.

TOTAL INFLUENCE

a. Read

b. Penetrate—Jet

c. Change gaps—Fire

d. Change gaps and penetrate—Jet Fire

e. Widen gap—Slant

This is how we run the Total Influence drills. We use seven chairs and a ball. We get the players to line up on the chairs. We call out a defensive call and they line up on the chairs. If I call 31 Jet the nose lines up in the 1 gap, the tackle lines up in the 3 gap. They step with the Jet foot and rip upfield. If we call 31 Fire Left they step laterally and change gaps. We make them go on the football. You can have one of the managers or injured players move the ball. We do not always go on the snap count. We will go on the snap of the ball and on the movement of the man. We stress the proper steps. This is how we start out teaching stunts.

Next we go to a two-on-one drill. We call a stunt and have him make the steps. We do not want to double-team block the man in this drill. This will help him learn to read people.

This is how we line them up. The tackle learns these techniques. He has a 1, 2, and a 3 on the guard. On the tackle he has to line up in the 5, 4 if he is reading the guard, and a 6, and outside the tackle is his base. If we put him on the center it is a Tom call. If the strike calls Left, he goes to the call side. He always goes with the strike.

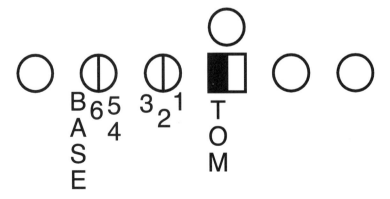

The nose line goes away from the strike. This is how he lines up. His base is on the center. He has a 1, 2, and a 3 position.

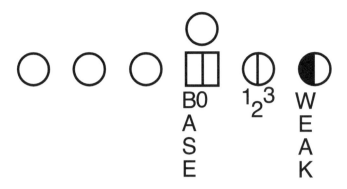

On the inside shoulder of the weak tackle we call it a weak call for the nose. He plays the same technique in a weak as he does in a 1 position. That is all it is for him. It is the same as a 3 position on the guard. It is the same if he is playing the center from the other side of the ball. That is his techniques.

Let me show you something about the 31 Stack. First, I want to show you how we teach the agilities. We stress feet, feet, feet. I think this is very important. We can't stress feet enough for those big guys. We run the Carioca, Rope, and Bag drills to work on the feet.

We do one on one every day during the season. We do hookups on every Tuesday and Wednesday. We go best against best. You do not need a ball carrier. We have linemen against linemen, one on one. The offensive coach calls his play and we call our defense. We only go for 10 minutes per day. We can go five Run and five Pass plays. That is the best way for us to get better; by going against good people on offense.

We run the dive drill. We put the ball down the middle in a 5-yard-wide chute. We change the positions around on defense and work on all of our calls.

We use the inside drill. I said Thud Pace here because it is Coach Curry's idea. We run this during the season. By Thud we mean we are not going to go full speed, except we do not pile on our good backs. We come up and put a shoulder on them and stop right there with them. We can run it as an eight-on-nine drill. This makes both sides of the ball more physical. We only run plays inside and the off-tackle plays.

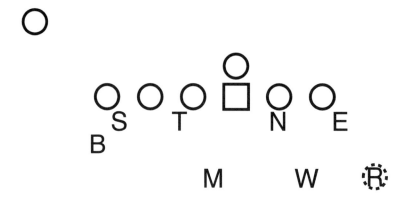

We can take the rover out of the drill if we want. We can work against the isolation, sprint draw, traps, and the fullback dive plays. The offense will sometimes run a sweep on you. We all know how the offensive people are in these drills. When they do that we want to make the sweep break outside on us in this drill. It is best against best.

Once we have taught 31 and Stack 5 we can make things interesting for them. We can line up and show the offense 31 and on the snap of the ball go to a Stack 5. We call Show Stack 5. We just move the strike, tackle, and nose over one gap. The end does not have to move.

Then we show them a Stack 5 and go to a 31 look on the snap of the ball. The strike, tackle, and nose move the other way a gap. Again, the end does not have to move. Now, we have a line moving back the other way. It is like a sickle cutting grass. The offense is trying to block a Stack 5 and you have gone back to a 31 look. That is tough on the offense. We did not run enough of these two stunts last year.

Chapter 6

DEFENSIVE LINE TECHNIQUES

Jim Heacock
Ohio State University
1997

I'm going to talk about defensive line play. There are four areas I'm going to hit on really quickly. I think the front four form the most critical part of any defensive unit. There are two things they have to do. They have to control the run and get pressure on the quarterback. I've been in this situation before. If you have to blitz to get pressure or stop the run, you will get burnt eventually. This year we had a front four that could get pressure. When we brought linebackers or the free safety, they created havoc in the backfield.

I think the next point is the most important thing. This is the thing I say most to the defensive line: Beat the blocker. That is the name of the game. The first thing a young defensive lineman wants to do is make a play. As coaches, we have to make them understand that if they want to make a play, they have to beat the blocker. That is the first thing I tell them. Someone is going to block you. Then I go through the offensive playbook. I show them in that book that they are not going to leave any linemen unblocked. That is where I start the progression.

There are three things that can happen to defensive linemen. They are going to use a base block, reach block, or cutoff block against him. If the defensive linemen can defeat the block, fight pressure, and get across pressure, that will take you to the ball, where you can make plays. The first thing that young lineman wants to do is to rise up to find the ball. He wants to make a play. The first thing he knows, the offensive lineman is blocking his butt off. The example is two boxers in the ring. If we are equal, and I'm not watching the other boxer, who is going to win the fight? The defensive lineman is going to get killed if his focus is on the quarterback or running back. The

61

offensive lineman's focus is on the defender. I have to get them to focus on the blocker.

If the guy across from you leaves, there is someone else coming to block you. He will get a down, fold, or trap block. Once the guy across from you leaves, the next guy coming is the guy the defender has to defeat. If it is a trap, he has to wrong-arm it and spill. If it is a down block, he has to get upfield or across the face. If he can beat the blocker, he can make plays.

Should a defender attack upfield or sit on the line of scrimmage and read? When I went to Bowling Green, we were strictly read defenders. We were in a parallel stance and were not going to get reached. When I went to Washington, I got more into getting upfield. Now we want to be able to do both. I'm convinced we have to do both. We have to be able to get up the field and come backdoor on all down blocks. We also have to be able to come cross-face on the line of scrimmage.

If I am a tackle over a guard who pulls, what do I do when the down block comes? In our game plan, we are going to have two ways of playing it. We are either going up the field and coming backdoor, or we are going across the face. If the offensive tackle knows the defensive tackle is attacking upfield, he takes a flat step to the line every time to get the defense walled off. But on the other hand, if the defensive tackle is always sitting on the line of scrimmage, the offensive tackle gets more depth on his charge.

What we teach is two calls. We have a red-and-green call. The green call is go. We are going upfield as hard as we can. If we get the down block, we are going backdoor. We grab cloth, swim, and come down the line of scrimmage behind the blocker.

If we have a red call, we sit on the line of scrimmage. If we get the down block, we strike and fight across face to get inside-out on the ball. Against Arizona State in the Rose Bowl, we always played red unless we were in a nickel defense. The reason for that was their counter play. They ran that play better than anyone I've seen. We wanted to stay on the line of scrimmage. Our 3 techniques made more plays than anyone because they thought he was coming upfield.

At Ohio State we basically have three fronts. We play the Bear front and the reduction to both sides. We call them slide, tight, and Ohio defense. Off each one of those defenses we have a frontline movement. That lets us change a gap for any defensive lineman. We have games to stunt the interior four defensive linemen. We also have blitzes off each one of those. This gives us a multiple look.

I know you guys don't want to listen to my philosophy, so I'll cover it quickly. It is not too different from most people's. But I do think this is important. I spend as much time with the players with this as I do with technique. One of the things we did this year was blitz a lot. Every time we blitzed, we twisted. I've never done that as much as we did this year. Our philosophy was to twist two down guys and tie up three guys trying to block them. Let me give you an example.

Let's take the nose guard and the 3 technique tackle. If we were coming with a Mike or Buck linebacker blitz, we twisted these two guys. We felt that if it took the two guards and the center to block the nose and 3 technique, no one was coming free. The only problem was the defensive linemen were not getting any sacks. That goes back to our first philosophical thought: The team comes first. We may not make the sacks, but the team does.

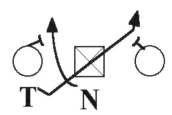

If you are going to play defensive line at Ohio State, you have to get after it. Activity is important for us. From when the ball is snapped until the whistle blows, these guys better be busting it. We do two things to help our activity. We are going to be in great condition, and we are going to keep fresh people in the game. If we have guys of equal ability, we will substitute more. We tell them to go three plays all out, and then we bring in the next guy, who does his three plays. This year we had four great players before there was a drop-off in talent. We didn't play our 2's very much. We went with the 1's. They had to be in great physical shape and very disciplined to the ball. The game that won us the Big Ten championship came at Indiana. We had a defensive end get up off the ground, pursue to the other side of the field, pick up a fumble, and return it for a touchdown. He actually picked the fumble up off an Indiana player's back and returned it.

The evaluation of a coach is whether his players improve. I always got a little nervous if I had a player who wasn't better the second game than he was the first. If he doesn't improve as the season goes on, that comes back to the coach. If you are working that kid every day with reps and techniques, he should get better. I emphasize that we have to get better every game and our last game better be our best.

Repetition is the name of the game. The more you can rep it, the better you are going to be. It is monotonous and boring. We try to use different drills to break it up. Our guys must see a reach block a thousand times. They see the down block a thousand times. We do it a million times if they need it.

We feel that we have to do a great job with adjustment. We have to adjust during a game. I can remember two games in my coaching career where we didn't do a good job of adjusting, and we lost the game. After we saw the film, it was too late. We have to adjust in advance in the game.

We were fortunate this year. We had guys who were students of the game. If they were not in class, they were watching tape of the opponents or their drill work. There is no excuse for missed assignments. I've been places where we had to prod those guys to get them to watch tape. They have to execute. They have to know what their assignment is and execute it. There is zero tolerance for making a mental mistake. I've never heard Coach Pagac yell at a guy for making a physical mistake, as long as it was aggressive.

Football is not going to be all good. You are going to have some adversity. Some things are going to go wrong during the course of a game. The last thing I need are guys coming off the field complaining. Against Purdue the first two times they had the ball, they threw two bombs. It was 0–14 before we knew it. I've been around some teams when things started to get hairy and panic set in. That is where I give Coach Pagac and Coach Cooper credit. They didn't panic. We had three quarters to play.

One of the biggest distractions you can have is players playing for you who are always in trouble. When I get together with my players, I tell them, "Here is the policy. I don't set them. They are Coach Cooper's policies. I work for him, these are his policies, and you are going to follow them. If you don't want to follow them, you don't play." You get that ironed out at the beginning. If not, you can have a coach-player problem when you have a game coming up. You don't need those distractions.

The last thing is this. I expect you to win and be excellent. If you want the same thing, then we will always be on the same page. You always have players who think that you are on them all the time. Just have them look at this philosophy. If they don't want the same thing, I'll get off them, but they won't play.

The next thing I want to do is go through what I call "10 vital techniques." If you are going to be a good defensive lineman, you better be able to do these 10 things. Number 1, and probably the toughest thing to do, is stance. Stance is number 1 in my opinion. You have to get in a good football stance. We start out with the flat back, toes upfield, and good balance. As the season goes on, players get lazy. A good stance will make you a better football player.

In our base stance, or red stance, we are heel to toe in stagger. We want 60 percent of our weight on our hands. I want their backs flat enough that I could eat dinner off them. However, I want the butt up a little.

If I get into the green stance, I want the stagger elongated. The hand is a little more in front. The feet are a little closer together. We are in a sprinter's stance somewhat. That lets us explode off the ball and get upfield.

The next thing is alignment. This is something we do a lot of. Basically, I have four alignments. I have what I call head, split, shade, and foot. The head is aligned head on head. The split is splitting the man right down the middle. That means the inside foot splits the crotch of the offensive man. The shade is my foot on his inside foot. I am not head up, but cheating a little to the outside. The last one is foot, which puts my inside foot on his outside foot. That is as wide as we get. This is a way to adjust the players' technique. If a player comes off and tells me he is getting reached, all I have to tell him is go to a foot alignment.

The distance off the line depends on the skill of a defensive lineman. The better he is, the closer he gets to the line. Our younger players start out back off the ball. That gives them time to read and keeps them from getting reached so easily.

The third thing is assignment. We call our two inside rushers power rushers. The two ends are speed rushers. We paint on our field our rush lanes. We run stunts and twists on these lines to make sure we stay in lanes as we rush the passer. I've seen a lot of great pass rushers who don't get too many sacks, but they get upfield in their lanes. That is what we emphasize. I start off with nothing but the bull rush. The pass-rush lane is their assignment.

The nose guard is the guy who gets beat up by the center and two guards in the pass rush. This year the nose guard could make a "me-you" call to the 3-technique tackle. That exchanged gaps and lanes in the pass rush. On the "you" call, the nose guard would step into the center-guard gap and then rush outside the guard. The tackle starts outside the guard, throws, and comes back inside in the face of the quarterback.

The fourth thing is get-off. This probably is the most important thing we do. We want the player's hand moving when the ball is moving. We have to get off on the football. That is the first thing we do in practice. We try to teach them to go on the movement of the ball, not sound. If you saw the Rose Bowl, we jumped on sound about three times, and I almost got fired. We watch the football.

We do a drill to work on this. A lot of the pro teams do this. We align our defensive linemen 5 yards away from the offensive linemen. All the offensive linemen do is backpedal. The defensive linemen sprint to them as fast as they can. They just tap them. We make a little game of it. The defense has to tap the offense before he gets 10 yards. The loser does up-downs. The whole idea is the get-off.

The strike-and-blow delivery defeats the offensive blocker. If the blocker weighs 320 pounds and the defensive player weighs 250 pounds, if you take him on square, he will beat your ass. We have to change the direction of the offensive blocker. That is where the bend in the knees and strike up through the target come into play. When we hit the sled, I do a jab-dip-rip drill. They take two steps and jab the bag. I say dip. They have to bend their knees down as far as they can go. I let them sit there for about five seconds. That gives them the feel of bending their knees. Then I say rip. They explode up through the sled.

We want to put our eyes in the V of the neck. That is our aiming point. We want shoulder pad under shoulder pad. We try to bring the hands under both armpits, bend the knees, explode up through the neck, and lock up. We have to stop him on the line.

After the blow delivery comes extension of the arms. That leads to number 6, separation from the block. The defensive lineman has to lock out his arm. It has gotten so bad with the holding calls. The referee calls holding once a game, and that is it. In our league we are getting held every play. When we run scout teams in practice, I tell them to hold our defense.

The seventh vital technique is disengagement. That is throwing the linemen away to get off the block. We work really hard on throwing the man. If you try to move before you disengage, the blocker will be right on you. We run a simple drill to practice this. I have a blocker in front of me. The defensive man has his hand under the armpits and locked out. All I do is step one way or the other. The defensive man throws the offense off the other way. It's a simple drill.

The eighth thing is pursuit. This year we did a cutup of every play that gained 10 yards or more against our defense. There were 27 plays in 11 games where the opponent gained 10 yards or more. Out of that 27, six were reverses, five of them were against our second team or others. That brings it down to maybe 17 plays in 11 games for 10 yards or more. I think that is pretty good. Our guys run to the football. We talk about relentless pursuit. We run a lot of pursuit drills. We constantly harp on it. The hardest thing I have to do is to get men on the line to run after a pass. To do this, the two most important things are attitude and effort.

The ninth thing is tackling. I'm not going to talk a lot about that. The one thing I will say is about fine-tune drills. We want to tackle a guy high from behind. That prevents a quarterback from throwing the ball, or it may cause a fumble. I do a drill at least once a week on this technique. Maybe it will happen in a game because I worked on it.

Another drill that is a fine-tuning drill is called the "bend drill." How many times have you seen a defensive end get a great pass rush, beat the blocker, but end up running by the quarterback because his momentum carried him wide? That is centrifugal force. We run a drill and time our ends on running around a cone and bending end. They have to dip their shoulder, touch grass, and run all the way around. We do it from both directions. That may be the skill that strips the ball from the quarterback.

One tackling drill I do every day is work on a quarterback breaking the pocket. I put a manager back behind a pass-rush drill. I use the quickest man I can find. We run our pass-rush drill, using our techniques to get free. Once we break free, the manager scrambles outside. I want them adjusting their paths and making an effort to get him. I don't want them to break free, break down, and sneak up on him. I want them coming hard. I call this the "brain drill" because as that defensive man is breaking free, I want him thinking that the quarterback is going to run somewhere. I don't want him to just rush upfield like a big lug. He has to think after he beats the block to get the quarterback.

These fine-tune drills are realistic. They are things that players are going to see in the games. I want them to have worked on them so they can handle them in the game.

The last thing is react to schemes. Every team that you play is going to be good at two or three schemes. We are going to identity the three or four things they do best. We are going to work like crazy on them that week in practice. Those are the 10 vital techniques we have to get across to our kids. When you put that all together, you have yourself a football player.

The most important part of the game to me right now is pass rush. You have to get pressure on the quarterback with your front four. I work four areas of pass rush. I work the get-off. That is the green stance. Next is the setup. This is the one I've tried to work on over the years. The next area is the move. You can use the rip, over, or bull rush. The last thing is the countermove. That is how I break down the pass rush.

Let me talk briefly about the setup. What we are trying to do is get you off balance. Every offensive coach in the country tries to keep his offensive linemen in a balanced frame all the time. When they are in that stance, they are good. It is hard to get around him when he is balanced up. We can't let him do that. For the first three series of every game, we are going to bull rush. The first thing I want that offensive lineman to do is to start to lean. If you hit that guy enough under his chin, he starts to lean into you. When he does, your pass-rush techniques are going to work.

When we bull rush, we have to feel the offensive linemen. I saw this in a 49ers camp. They blindfold their pass rushers. The offensive blocker retreats in the bull rush. At some point the offensive lineman has to make a stand to keep from being pushed back into the quarter-back. When he locks back and leans into the defense is when we pull him forward and go around him. We don't use the blindfold, but we do close our eyes. It is the feel they have to recognize. The setup is the bull rush, which is designed to get the guy leaning forward.

With our 3 technique and nose guard, we use a head fake. All they do is jab to the outside, club to the inside, and rip underneath. We are trying to move the offensive linemen's weight to one side or the other. In the power rush, we work the offensive linemen to the outside of our pass lane, then rip and come inside. We do these things within the confines of our lanes.

Pass rush is attitude, effort, and toughness. Football is a physical game. We always look for those types of guys.

In the drill is where you have to be creative. This is where football gets boring. I have never had a player who liked individual drills. They want to scrimmage. The first drill that I like to use is a pass-rush drill. This is a toughness drill. Sometimes I have trouble with the head coach over this drill because it gets out of hand at times. I want to find out how tough he is, whether he wants to get to the quarterback, and whether he won't give up. It is also a good conditioning drill.

The drill has two offensive blockers on one pass rusher. The first lineman engages the defensive rusher at the line of scrimmage. The second blocker waits in reserve. If the rusher gets past the first blocker, he has to take on the second blocker. The first man now drops in back to take on the rusher again. The drill continues until the rusher gets to the quarterback or the whistle blows. If the rusher gets there, the offense has to do 20 up-downs. You can tell a lot about your players from this drill.

In this next drill I have an offensive man on a defensive man. I use two dummies and two backs on each. The ball carrier is in the tailback position. All blocks are base blocks. I point to the back who I want to carry the ball. On the snap of the ball, the offensive man tries to block the defensive man's butt off. The back runs through the bags. The defensive man has to use his vital techniques to get to the ball carrier. The first thing he has to do is neutralize the blocker. In the beginning, most of the defenders are trying to see which back is coming. They are not focused on the blocker and end up in my lap.

The first thing you are going to find out is where that defender is looking. I tell the offense that holding is legal, so he grabs the defender. If the offense can hold him, he didn't lock out. The young guy finally gets the lockout completed and goes for the tackle. The offensive man will bury him, because he did disengage. You can see all the mistakes from the results that occur. This drill teaches the progression to the tackle. We don't put the backs on the ground. We form tackle.

I can stand behind the drill and see all the vital techniques. We videotape this drill. The biggest problem they all have is trying to watch the ball carrier. This probably is the best drill we do. It covers everything.

I adjust the depth of the backs and the width of the dummies to the skill of the players. For the younger players, I tighten the dummies and move the ball carrier back. With our older players, I challenge them. I put the dummies wider and the backs closer. I determine that by how happy I am or how much I want them to do well or not so well. With the young guys, the ball carriers are about 8 yards deep. The great defensive linemen that I've had fight pressure naturally. They are instinctive. Wrestlers are good at that. I love to coach wrestlers on the defensive line because they have a knack for fighting pressure.

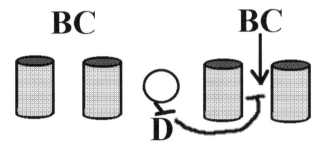

The next drill I use is a repetition drill, working on schemes. I line up the guys across the field with offense on one side and defense on the other. I stand behind the defense and give them commands. I tell them they have their left arm free. They take two steps, getting the pad under pad. I check each of them as they go. It is rapid-fire. In the course of five minutes I can get through base, reach, and cutoff blocks.

After that I work on low blocks. I work on everything that might happen to them in a game. Then we go to stunts. I tell them they have their left arm free, slant right. I coach the offense to do certain things to the defense. I tell them to scoop on their steps and watch the reaction of the defense. Then I line them up and we pass-rush. So in five to 10 minutes I can get in all the situations that they see in a game.

This drill goes along with the bend drill. I put them on the line. They have to sprint upfield, bend around the cone, and dive on the dummy. I time this to see how fast they can get it done. There is nothing wrong with diving. They come around the horn and dive in on the dummy. That forces them to angle in.

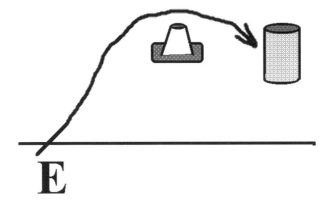

E

When we play the low block, I want the eyes of the defensive line-men down on the blocker. What they want to do is hit them on the back. That is being lazy and not wanting to bend their knees. I want the hands in front of them, keeping him away from their feet. If the defensive guy is focused on the ball carrier, he'll get cut. If the blocker goes down, the defender goes down with him.

We don't see the double-team block much any more. The block we are seeing is the chip off to the linebacker. If the defender drops to the ground on a chip block, that is what the offense wants him to do. We stay on our feet until we feel pressure coming.

We don't break down when we tackle. If we break down on a good back, it won't make any difference. We probably aren't going to make the tackle anyway. I tell them to go get them. If we miss, make them readjust their movement. We are going to attack everyone. The only thing different is that the second guy in strips the ball. Our approach is to attack and go make it happen.

Let me show you the three fronts we run. This first one is the re-duced front weak side. We shade the nose guard to the weak side. The ends are in a 5 and a 7 technique. The tackle plays a 3 technique to the tight-end side.

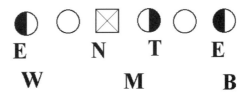

We play with the Will linebacker to the weak side, the Mike linebacker in the middle, and the Buck linebacker to the tight-end side.

Our best run defense was what we called "tight." We played the
nose in a strong shade to the tight end. The tackle played a 2 technique to the split-end side. Our strongside defensive end was in a 4
technique, and the weak side was in a 5 technique. The Will linebacker played on the tight end. The Mike linebacker played a 3 technique strong. The Buck linebacker played a 2 stack to the weak side.
The tackle slanted into the A gap weak. Mike and Buck linebackers
fast-flowed to the strong side, and the free safety played the weakside B gap for the cutback. That was our first-and-10 defense.

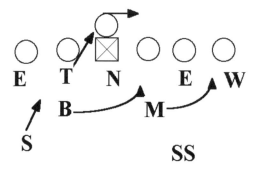

The Bear defense is probably our best defense. We played this a ton
in the bowl game. As far as making things happen, this is our best
defense. We have a good front five who got off on the ball. We twist
our inside people and blitz like crazy from this. We played man-free in
the secondary. The other thing we did off this was to show the Bear,
drop out, and play zone. We slanted back to the strong side, and the
defense ended up being the tight front. The Will linebacker would
drop, and we played zone out of it. In the bowl game we played this
with our nickel defense.

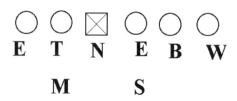

Chapter 7

DEFENSIVE END TECHNIQUES

Glynn Jones
University of Louisville
1997

The Louisville defense has been ranked among the top 25 nationally in scoring defense in each of the past two seasons, including a number 7 finish in 1995. In the last 22 games, the defense has allowed an average of 16.8 points per game. This past season, our defense held opponents to an average of 235.8 yards per game, good for fifth among NCAA Division I teams.

We held opponents to 96.7 yards per game in pass-efficiency defense to finish 13th overall on defense. We stress stopping the run at Louisville. We talk each day about how to stop the run. We stress this to our kids, and we have been successful in doing that. We allowed opponents an average of 81.1 yards per game on the ground to finish fourth nationally.

Our defense had a school-record 45 sacks in 1996. Senior defensive end Carl Powell had 11. Seven of the sacks came in a two-week period against Memphis and North Carolina. I will talk about some of the defensive techniques he used to get those sacks.

Next I want to share with you our defensive goals for the year. What do you want to do to be successful? We keep the goals on a chart and keep them updated after each game. This is what we wanted to achieve in 1996.

1996 Defensive Team Goals

Each of these headings is listed at the top of the chart. What we feel we need to do to win is listed under the heading. We have our schedule down the side of the chart, and we fill the columns in as the season progresses.

Win

- Points allowed.

- Hold opponent to 14 points per game.

Rush Defense

- Hold opponent to 150 yards or less per game.

- Hold opponent to 3.3 yards average per game.

Pass Defense

- Hold opponent to 150 yards or less per game.

- Hold opponent to 6.0 yards average per attempt.

- Hold opponent to under 60 percent completion per game.

Turnovers

- Cause three or more fumbles per game.

- Turn the ball over at least two times per game.

- Turn the ball over to the offense at least one time on the plus-50-yard line.

- Intercept one out of every seven pass completions.

Total Defense

- Hold opponents to 300 yards total offense per game.

- Hold opponent to 33 percent or less 3rd down efficiency.

- No runs over 15 yards.

- No passes over 25 yards.

You can see the areas where we did well and the areas where we did not do well. We use these goals to set up our defense for the season. We stress to our defense that we must get to the football. We ask them this question. What must we do to win? This is what we came up with.

How we will win on defense? Do not allow a long pass completion for a touchdown. Do not allow a long run for a touchdown. Intercept passes and return them for yardage and touchdowns. Force the opponent to fumble.

We stress the fact we must play great goal-line defense. We feel that if we can do that, we have a chance to win. We stress fundamentals on defense. This is what we stress with our players:

1) Shoulders square.

2) Proper arm free.

3) Pads over our toes.

4) Keep a base.

5) Don't run around the blocker.

6) Do not give them anything but pads, bones, and elbows.

7) Stay on your feet.

We start with our general techniques. We start every thing from a base. This is what we stress: stance, alignment, key ball to man, responsibility.

This past year we played three different defensive fronts. The first defense we teach is what we call our load 53 defense. We have a tackle call to the tight-end side. The tackle and end to the tight end are going to line up in a 3 technique and a 7 technique. On the split-end side we have a tackle in a shade technique and the end in a 5 technique. Our Sam linebacker goes to the tight-end side. The Mike linebacker is on the outside shoulder of the center. The Will linebacker is stacked inside the offensive tackle and behind our 5-technique end. As you can see, we are based out of the 4-3 alignment. That is our base defense. We do a lot of other things out of this defense.

Load 53

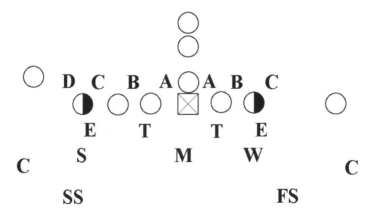

The next defense we look at is the over 53 look. Our call-side end is in a 9 technique, and the backside end is in a 5 technique.

Over 53

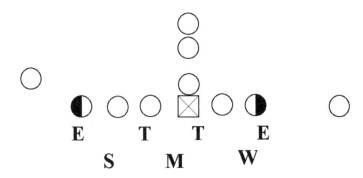

Between the load and over calls, only two players changed their techniques. The only two people to change are the call-side end and the Sam linebacker. The end steps out to a 9 technique, and the Sam linebacker steps inside. If we call *load,* the call-side end knows he is in the 7 technique. If we call *over,* the end is in a 9 technique.

We are a one-gap defense up front. The tackles are going to work together. The tackles know that if we are in load, the offside tackle is responsible for the B gap and the backside tackle is responsible for the A gap. The ends know that if we call load, the call-side end is responsible for the C gap. He is a C-gap player.

Our linebackers are responsible for two gaps. They have a primary gap and a secondary gap. In our load, the Mike linebacker is an A-gap player. The Sam linebacker is a D-gap player, and the Will linebacker is a B-gap player. We are a four-spoke secondary. We have two safeties and two corners. We will always give you that look. If we go to our over 53, the look will stay the same for our secondary. What we are doing is nothing hard. We try to keep everything simple. Those are the two fronts we ran against pro action. If the offense came out in two backs, one tight end, and two receivers, we call that look *regular personnel.* When we see that set, that is what you are going to get from our defensive front. If you come out in what we call H formation, which is two tight ends with one back and two wide receivers, we get into more of a base look.

When we call load G, this tells the backside tackle he is going to move from a shade to a 2 technique. Our backside end is in a 5 technique. This is good against the bootleg reverse. I will cover that later.

On the isolation play, the offside tackle is going to get a drive block. The first block that the end has to learn to defeat is the drive block. He has to step up and knock the tackle upfield. He keeps his outside leg and arm free and forces the ball inside.

5 Technique vs. Drive Block

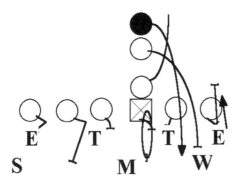

The fullback is going to lead on the Will linebacker. He steps up and takes on the fullback with his inside arm and leg. He forces the ball back inside for the Mike linebacker. The Mike linebacker is playing two gaps. He is responsible for the strong-side A gap, and he is also responsible for the backside B gap on flow away.

I want to talk about two drills that I do that help the ends take care of the men in front of them. The first drill I will talk about is our explosion drill. We have to be able to attack that man in front of us. He needs to know what to do if that offensive tackle knocks him off the ball. He has to be able to step back and strike again.

We start off in a two-point stance with a slight bend in our ankles, knees, and hips. The head is up. As the man steps toward me, all I want to do is explode and put my face mask inside with my head up and get my hands inside on the breastplate. If you have a two-man sled, you can use it to work on the drill. If you do not have a sled, take a player and have him hold a hand dummy. Teach him to explode into the dummy. Teach him to strike a blow in a good football position. We call this pads-out drill.

We want to teach them to come up with the ankles, knees, and hips and explode into the man and push him off of me. We want to teach him to play with pads up. He has to learn to step up and hit the blocker and knock him back off the ball. All you need is three or four reps a day working on pads-out. It is best to start the drill with a stationary machine. He does not need to move his feet. You are looking for explosion and the power move.

We teach the drill a little differently than most people. Most people start from a three-point stance. We start out teaching this technique from a two-point stance. Once he learns to hit the sled and to explode and get his knees and hips into the drill, we teach him to step up and strike from a three-point stance. We call this our pads-out drill.

We have a defensive checklist. There are a lot of things to teach the defensive ends. We do not make this list very difficult. This is very simple. It is a good thing for me to review. Each day I go over certain drills. I do not do everything on the checklist. We do some of these drills every day. We talk about these drills from the two-, three-, four-, and six-point stance.

Next, I want to talk about the skate drill. In this drill we do basically three things:

1) Lock out and separate.

2) Lock out and rip.

3) Lock out and beat the reach block.

I start the defensive end in a good football position. His hands should be on the outside to start out. We always talk about hand and eye placement. We want the hands inside on the breastplate. His palm is up, and we are in the V of the neck. If we have inside gap, we only work on one thing. We pull with the inside arm and lock out with the outside arm. We just turn the shoulders.

After that, we need to go upfield with the man. We pull on the outside and lock out. As we do that, we are putting a step into the move. It is a quick step. We are trying to get the players to understand leverage on the blocking. After doing some research, I found out that our kids need to know and understand pressure points and leverage to play good football.

The next phase of the drill is lock out and rip. We do the same as before, but now we rip and come upfield 3 yards. We want to keep the shoulders square. We run the drill so each player gets one or two shots on it.

The next drill is against the reach block. Now we want him to lock and reach. He is in a good football position, and he is inside. The offensive man has already reached the defensive man. The football is going to the outside. Now we want to pull the man back inside. We want to use his weight and leverage. We want to throw him back inside and get off the block. If you are playing the 5 technique, you do not know where the offensive man is going. You must react to what he is doing.

5 Technique vs. Reach Block

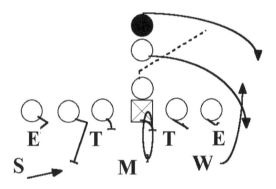

Let me go back to the basic drive block again. As the offensive man comes at our end, he is in a three-point stance. My inside foot is going to be on his outside foot. I have to step up on him. We hit him in the V of the neck, keep the hands inside, and drive him back upfield. If you get movement and knock him back upfield, then the offense does not have a chance. You are forcing the ball inside. We do not want them going inside too quickly. We know that tailback can squirt back outside. We know all linebackers are going to scrape to the ball.

On the Toss Sweep, the 5-technique end must make his first step upfield. He has to know how to react against that blocker. That blocker is trying to get to his outside number. We want to string the play out wide. We do not want the ball going north and south. We have the safety who is going to fill inside. Also, we have a Will linebacker who is going to fill. We want our end to get outside and make the play.

The next block we are going to see against our 5 technique is the down block. This is the block we see on the inside zone play. I want the end to step upfield with that first step. He sets his feet with the second step. This gets him going. He wants to keep his shoulders square. The offensive tackle blocks down inside. I tell our ends to choke down and to find out what is going on. I want him to drag that back leg two steps. If the ball is inside, the end reads the mesh point for that quarterback. His eyes should be on that quarterback. The quarterback is going to give the ball to the fullback, or he is going to keep the ball on the bootleg, or it is going to be a reverse play. Most teams like to run the zone play and cut back into the C gap. We want to take that away from the man with the ball. As the blocker steps down, we want to step up. We want to punch the tackle inside. Now we are going to drag our feet and keep our shoulders square to the line of scrimmage. They can see everything from this position. I tell them to train their eyes to keep the shoulders square. The first thing he should expect is the full-back on the inside zone play.

5 Technique vs. Down Block

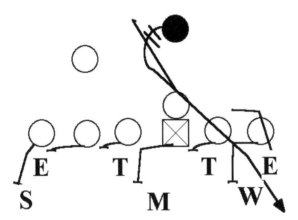

The first person we tell the end to look for is the pulling lineman coming down the line. If the offensive lineman is off the line, it will probably be some kind of bootleg or waggle play. If he sees that, he heads upfield to try to contain the quarterback. If the man is pulling down the line, we want our end to occupy the hole and squeeze the play down. We want to attack the inside shoulder of the blocker and push him back upfield. This will allow our Will linebacker to scrape over the top and make the stop. If our defensive end does not get under the pulling guard, we have trouble.

Down Block/Kick-Out/Counter

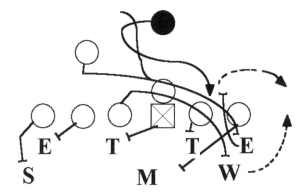

That allows the tackle to get down on the Mike linebacker. They have a chance to get the play away. Will is going to scrape off outside. The Mike linebacker is filling inside and plays the football.

The next play that the 5 technique looks for is the bootleg reverse. If the fullback does not have the ball, he looks for the reverse. We ask our end to keep his shoulders square to the goalpost. We want him to make a straight line and get up the field. We do not want him to try to get outside. We want him to go straight upfield. We want to make the football bounce wide. We want to make the football bounce deeper and wider. Hopefully, we will have some help, and they will make the play. We want to make the ball bounce deep and wide and let our pursuit catch the ball. If we can do that, we will be in good shape.

Those are the reads we do every day in practice for the 5 technique. This is the bread and butter of playing defensive end. We do not switch our ends. We play the techniques the same.

5 Technique—Bootleg Reverse

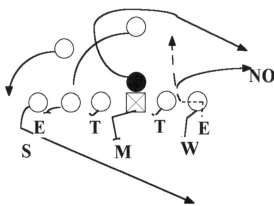

The next thing I want to talk about is our 7 technique. I feel that we play the 7 technique pretty well. Again, the inside hand is down, and the outside foot is back. He lines up on the inside neck of the tight end. Everything we talk about starts with that first step. The tight end comes off to drive-block the 7 technique. We do the same things that we did against the offensive tackle when we were in the 5 technique. We want to step up and use our hands to get inside the V of his neck and drive him back up the field. We key inside. Some teams key the offensive tackle. We feel that the tight end will tell us what is going on. There are only three or four things he can do. He can reach inside to try to cut us off, he can drive-block us, he can release outside on a pass route, and he can sit back and block for some type of play like the draw. If our end can understand the progression and know what is coming off, he will be in good shape.

Again, it is the same as the 5 technique against the tackle on the drive block. We want to step up, punch, get our hands inside, and lock the tight end out. We want to find out what is going on with the ball. If the football is inside, we want to close off the C gap. He is a C-gap player.

7 Technique vs. Counter

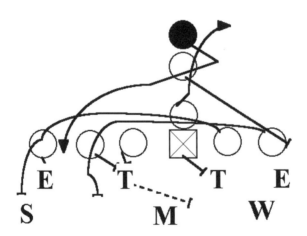

Let's go on to the zone play. The next big read he is going to get is the counter off tackle. This was a big read for us this year. The tight end would step up and get our end into a drive block. He would punch to the inside. As he was doing that, the offensive tackle was taking a zone step to get outside of our end so he could reach him. That is a tough block for the tackle, especially if the end is a player.

We want our end to explode and make a straight line up the field. We want to attack the end as he releases. We do not want him to release to get to our Sam linebacker. We try to hold him up from going inside. If we can do that, it will take the tackle and end to block our end. Our Sam linebacker can make the play on a scrape to the outside. Also, our Mike linebacker is scraping to that side. The zone play may go 5 yards outside. If we can make the play go back inside, we are happy. If the play stretches outside, the C gap also stretches. The same is true for the B and A gaps as they stretch. Everyone has to get into their gaps and stretch the play. As the play cuts back, the pursuit will make the play.

7 Technique vs. Outside Zone

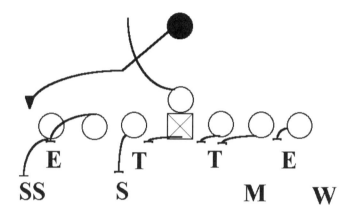

The next thing I want to talk about is playing the draw and screen plays. Every day we talk to our ends about these plays. If that offensive tackle gives our end a high hat and the tackle tries to punch him upfield and opens his hips, he knows something is wrong. We need to learn how to play the draw. As the end comes off the ball, most tackles are going to hunch back and try to knock the end upfield. I tell the end that he has to stop in his tracks. If he sees the tackle and sees the draw, he has to retrace his steps and come back down inside and make the play. If our end does get upfield and then he sees the draw, we want him to retrace his steps straight back down the field. If he can do that, he probably will make the tackle at the line of scrimmage, or the play may bounce outside.

Next, I want to talk about what I call all of the unusual plays that the defensive end is going to see from a 7 technique. This is something you have to put into your practices and work on. We work on the screen with our 5 and 7 technique. If the tackle tries to chop us as we get upfield and the quarterback continues to give ground, then something is going on. The end has to develop some instincts. If he feels that the screen is developing, he must get downfield. We want to plant and move our eyes to the outside. We are looking for a receiver coming back down inside. He may be able to break the play up if he can get there in time, or he may be able to make the tackle as soon as the receiver catches the ball.

We work on the draw and screen every day. We take a football and have them in their positions. We simulate the quarterback on a drop. If the quarterback drops the ball down, we have them step and plant the inside foot and open back to the inside. He retraces his steps, looking back inside. We want him in position to make the play. If the quarterback drops deeper, the defender should know it is a screen. One of the first plays we are going to check for is the screen. If the outside screen is not there, we look for the middle screen. We work this drill every day. In the course of the game, when they run the screens, you have to be able to react to them. Because we have covered what to do, we feel we have a chance to be successful.

Next, I want to talk about the pass rush. The thing we want to do is to key the football and movement. We are in a three-point stance. When we are in the pass-rush mode, we want to close our base stance. We use more of a sprinter's stance. We tell him to get into the most comfortable stance. We want him to be able to rush upfield. We want him to be able to rush the quarterback. We want our rush people to know the down and distance on each play. We want them to attack half the man as they get upfield. We always want to have a game play. I tell our players that we have a first move and then we have a countermove. I am going to go over three types of pass rushes, the rip, swim, and spin techniques.

The first technique I will cover is the speed rush. It is third and 10, and we have to get to the quarterback. I want the end out wide in a sprinter's stance. I ask our end to get to 3 yards right behind the offensive tackle. We can run by the tackle for that 4-yard stretch. We can beat the tackle to that point. If we can beat them on the speed rush, we can get to the quarterback. That is the speed rush. Use your speed to beat the blocker.

Next, we talk about attacking one half of the man. If the tackle gets to the spot and we get tied up with him, we want to be able to beat him. Once the blocker gets his shoulders turned, you have something you can work with. We work on the outside half of the man. What I am talking about is basically a rip move. We step with the outside foot, rip with the inside arm, step through the man, and go get the quarterback.

The next move we talk about is the swim move. I bring the arm up and bring the elbow up inside. This will clear you, and you can get to the quarterback.

We have the tackle so concerned because we have beaten him to the outside. Next, we want to get to the bull-rush move. We get our face mask into the man and drive him back into the quarterback. The feet never stop moving. I want them to perfect their moves and be able to use their best move in a game.

The next move is the spin move. As we make contact, we want to take the inside foot and step up and then spin. As we spin, we want to make sure that we are by the man. If you don't, he can step back inside and pick you up. The spin move and countermoves have been good for us.

I will go over three pass-rush stunts. We do not do a lot of different stunts on the pass rush. First is what we call the Texas stunt. The tackles penetrate first, stepping inside and then slanting outside into the face of the offensive man. The ends are going to come down inside. They come off the inside hip of the tackles. This should free him up to the quarterback.

Pass Rush—Texas

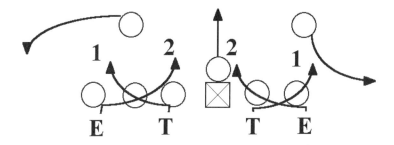

On the Ex stunt the ends go first, and the tackles come outside off the hips of the ends.

Pass Rush—Ex

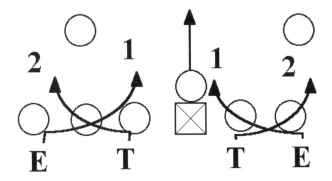

The stunt that was very effective for us was what we called Taco. We have a Texas on the call side, and we have an Ex on the split side. This is good against man protection. We have an end in the A gap and one in the B gap.

Pass Rush—Taco

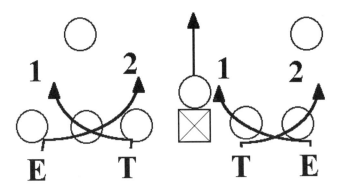

That is all of our pass-rush stunts. Most of our sacks came off the base rush.

Chapter 8

DEFENSIVE LINE TECHNIQUES

Greg Karpinsky
University of Cincinnati
1998

We are an Eight-Man-Front Defense. We are a pressure, get-after-it type defense. Today most offenses want to throw the ball all over the place. Still, our number 1 mandate is that we must be able to stop the run. If you can stop teams on the run you can be successful.

There are really three types of running. People run the ball at the line of scrimmage with their running back. Also, teams have to stop the run after the catch on a pass. People are not going to beat you by just throwing the ball all over the place. But 5-yard routes that turn into 30-yard gains will kill you. The third run you must stop is the quarterback scramble. Those are the three things we pride ourselves on at Cincinnati.

Along those lines we want to try to confuse the offense. We like to show the offense multiple looks. We are going to move our people around by using the stems. Also, we want to show a Blitz look on every snap. We are going to put eight men up near the line of scrimmage. It does not mean we are going to bring all of them on every down. On the snap we are going to bring six men. We may bring an extra man in the box and bring everyone.

Our goal is to stop the run. Last year we were fifth in the country against the run. We gave up 84.5 yards per game. In our last three games, teams averaged about 55 passes per game against us. They just flat-out refused to run against us.

One thing we pride ourselves on is that we will play hard. We want to be the best pursuit team in America. Our guys really believe this. A lot of people say you can't coach pursuit. I disagree with that. It is not natural for a defensive tackle to put his hand on the ground and

87

then go chase the quarterback all over the field. It has to be ingrained in them down after down. We are going to play hard and we are going to coach pursuit. We run drills to teach pursuit and we want our guys busting their butts to get to the ball. We want 11 guys flying to the football on every snap.

We want to lead the country in take-aways. Last year we forced 30 turnovers. That put us in the top 10 in the country. We had 18 fumbles and 12 interceptions for 30 turnovers.

We are a Gap Control defense. Our ends will play 3, 5, and 9 techniques. They play the outside shades on people. We may show you a 6 on the tight end and a 4 head up on the tackle. We will play some inside shade in the 7 technique and the 4 "I" technique. In our base look we show you an Eight-Man Front. We walk up our Strong Safety and we move our linebackers up on every play. We try to get our Sam and Mike up on every play. Our ends initially play a 7 technique and on the weak side we may show a 4 technique, but we are really in a 4 "I" technique. This is our Base Look.

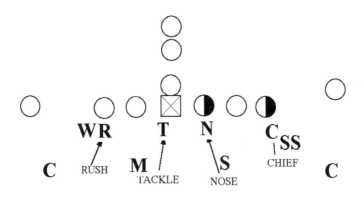

I firmly believe you must teach your kids what the offense can do to you. You have to teach them personnel. Is there one tight end in the game or two tight ends in the game? How many running backs do they have in the game? I am a firm believer in this because it dictates what the offense can do to you. If the offense sends out two tight ends and one back with two wide receivers, they can only run so much. There are just so many plays you can run out of each set. Players must understand this. It dictates how we will play.

We label our ends the Rush End and the Chief End. The Chief goes to the Call side. He goes with the Nose man. Our Rush and Tackle go together. A lot of this is based on personnel. The backfield set dictates how we are going to play our end. We play our basic alignment about 70 percent of the time. It is a good run defense. If we are anticipating pass we do not want to be a little wider.

The other look we use is a 46 look. You can set the defense Strong or you can set it Weak. You can base it on your personnel. We put the Chief in a 3 technique inside. We are going to play 3's, 5's, and 9's with the ends. We will play some inside shades in the 4 "I" and the 7 technique.

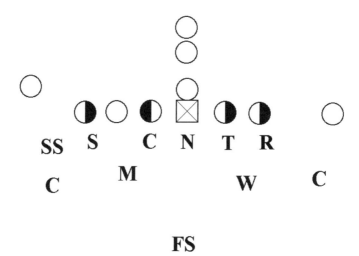

I want to talk about the way we structure our practice. Basic fundamentals still win football games. I am talking about tackling, pursuit, and attacking the line of scrimmage. We set up our practice schedule to give us a chance to work on these fundamentals. We take about 20 minutes per day on individual drills.

Coach Minter is a firm believer in group drills. Every day during the season we are going to be in pads twice a week and we are going to line up and do group drills. We line up and the drill is segmented. We go with the defensive end against tight ends and tackles. The inside defensive players go against the center and guards. We work against our offense. We work on specific drills. We work good on good for 10 minutes on those two days. Everyone gets good work against good players. We line up and go at it in pads for 10 minutes. We work on the inside runs. It is a tough drill.

In our individual practice we work on our pursuit drill every day. The first thing when the defense gets together is to work on pursuit for five minutes. Last year we did a drill called "Three and Out." Also, we ran a Sideline Pursuit Drill and an Interception Pursuit Drill. We go three in a row teaching our kids pursuit. We do work on a little conditioning as we go hard three or four plays in a row. We stress "Three and Out" for every series.

The next thing we did was to run a drill that we called "Rick's Rules." It was a Fundamental Circuit that we used. In each circuit we had a variety of ways to emphasize different fundamentals. One day it may be tackling. For three or four minutes everyone on our team tackles. We may go three or four minutes working on delivering a blow. It may be in a one-on-one drill or it may be on a sled. Everyone runs the drill, regardless of the position played on defense. Next we do some type of footwork over bags. Then we do some type of cut and skate drill. We work on a lot of fundamentals in the drills.

In addition to that we run a Turnover Circuit. We emphasize the Force category and we emphasize a Recovery category. We have three or four stations going at once. In the Force Drills we work on stripping the ball. We run a Tomahawk Drill which is coming off the edge. We cover how to attack the quarterback and how to strip the ball and how to secure the tackle.

In the Recover Drill we work on some type of Scoop-and-Score Drill. We work on picking the ball up and scoring. We work on getting on the ball and actually secure the ball. We also did some type of Interception Drill. Every Thursday we did some type of ball drill for the linemen. Some of you may think I am crazy but we do it. How many times do linemen get a chance to catch a screen pass? In the last two years we have had linemen drop tipped balls. They bobbled the ball because they were not used to catching it. We want our defensive linemen to get used to handling the ball so it is not foreign to them. A lot of times a ball is loose on the ground near the sideline and they try to fall on the ball and knock it out of bounds. You have to work on the drill so it becomes natural for them to pick it up and go with it.

When I get started on individual work it depends on which circuit we are doing first. After the Circuit Drills we are going to do some type of footwork. We do it every day. You have to do footwork with the big guys. We work with ropes and bags. We run some type of drill where they have to pick their feet up and down. Then we will combine a bag drill with a cut drill.

Next we work on Delivering a Blow everyday. We can't emphasize it enough. The line has the only positions in football where you have to hit someone every down. Defensive backs and linebackers may not hit anyone on some plays. If you play up front every single down you have to take someone on.

Everything we do is taught in progression. We start by teaching them Blow Delivery. We start if they do not know anything about it. We start out one on one. They line up in a four-point stance. They are working on quick hands and getting the head up. We talk about leading with the eyes. If you get your eyes up, your head will come up. We work on the different techniques on the One-on-One Drill.

Next we may get on the sled. We may get on a wall. We have pads on the wall. We work on stepping and punching. How many times have you gotten two players across from each other and all they want to do is wing it? They do not want to step. We put them across from another player, across from a sled, and against the wall. The first step is a punch. In 30 seconds you can do right foot first, left foot first, then punch. You can get all of your group included in that time.

Another thing we do is to work on some type of Separation in the Press Drill. When you come off a block you must get separation. You must see what it feels like to get separation. We do a simple little drill to help with separation. We put our defensive line down on all fours. We are going to be shaded a little. I have the blocker physically lean into the defensive man. If I am on defense I want to feel the weight of the blocker. I want to work my hips and I want to work on separation. I get the blocker in tight and then I bench press him away from my body. We may have them do 10 of those moves. It is a simple bench press drill. You work hips, and you keep your elbows tight.

We cannot do all of these drills every day. We may do the bench press on days when we are not doing a lot of heavy work.

Everyone talks about the hands in playing defense. "Get your hands up; get your hands inside." If your elbows are away from your body you expose your chest to the blocker. We tell them to keep the elbows in close to their body. If the elbows get away from your body there is no way you can keep the offensive man from getting into your chest. We have a one-man sled and we use it a couple of times a week. It is a one-man leverage pad. If you do not have a one-man sled you can use the three-man sled or the seven-man sled. It is the same thing. We are going to come off and we are going to attack the sled. We come underneath on contact and keep our elbows inside and make the punch. He does not want to stop the knee action. Now, how many times have you seen a lineman get into the man and make his punch and then stop? That is because he stops his knees. As you come off the punch, raise your knees. We are going to beat him to the neutral zone. That is our goal. We want to beat him at the line and get to the neutral zone. We want to keep a good base and keep the toes pointed north and south. Don't just stop the knees.

The other thing I have touched on is our Takeoffs. We emphasize takeoffs. We want to get off the line of scrimmage and get into the man. We want to explode into him from a three-point stance. We stress eyes, hands, and shoulder pads. We want to keep the elbows by our side. Protect your chest.

We are going to talk a little about our stance. We are in a sprinter's-type stance. We are a little elongated. We have a tight, narrow base. I want to get my hand about three inches outside my head. I can crowd the ball, but how many times have you see them go over the line of scrimmage and get the head in the neutral zone? I try to put my hand about three inches out in front of my head. Now I can line up a little easier on the ball. We teach you near hand down as far as our alignment purposes.

If I am in a 7 technique against a tight end I want to put my eyeball on the offensive man's breastplate. Some of this is dictated by backfield sets and by splits. That is my initial aiming point. I put my near foot to the blocker back. I am in a sprinter's stance and I am coming off the ball and attack him. My keys are to my man to the near back. It does not matter if I am in a 5 technique or 7 technique, the keys do not change. It is near man, near back.

The kind of split will dictate the kind of blocking scheme we are going to get. Chances are the wide man may be releasing. As soon as the man disappears I am going to let him go. If his breastplate disappears from me I start looking for my near back. If I get a tight split I will become more run conscious. I will be a little heavier on my key. We have a visual key and a pressure key everywhere we are lined up.

If you are playing a 7 technique on the left side, the tight end is going to be your visual key. That is the man you are watching. The offensive tackle is the next nearest man. He is your pressure key. You are going to feel him.

The other things we teach are the escapes. I think it is important to teach kids how to get off blocks. How many times do you hear coaches yell at kids to go make the play. The kid must understand how to get off the block. You have to teach that to them. It is not natural.

Everyone does the one-on-one or Oklahoma drill at the beginning of practice in the fall. Initially you start off with two linemen and a back. Some teams just start with two linemen. That is the way we do it. We line them up to see who can kick the other man's tail. It becomes a defensive drill because it becomes a stalemate. They are struggling like heck against each other.

Then we add the back to the drill. Now who starts winning the drill? The offensive linemen. Before, the defensive linemen did not have to worry about the back. Now, with the back he must look for the back. They forget to defeat the blocker and concentrate where the back is. They forget their technique. This is something you must teach.

I firmly believe we must teach them how to get off the blocks. It all starts with explosion and separation. They must get their hips in the hole. He has a gap he is responsible for. He must get his hips in the hole. If his hips are in the hole he can't be reached. It gives him an easier chance to get off the block. This all starts with a normal teaching progression. He must understand how to attack the blocker. He must know what it feels like to get separation. That is where the bench press drill comes into play. After he gets separation he must get his hips in the hole.

When we talk about getting the hips in the hole we want a good fit. From this point he must understand how to get off the block. We tell them to never walk away from a block. If I start walking, the blocker keeps reach blocking. He must know how to get off the block. We start with a normal teaching progression. We go back to the bench press. The blocker is not moving. All he is doing is leaning into me. I get the blocker fit, and then I am going to get my hips in the hole. We want to use the Push-Pull Technique. I want to get the blocker's shoulders turned but I also want to get my outside arm locked out if I can. It is not always possible to lock it out. If I get him locked out and my hips are in the hole, now it is a piece of cake. The key is to keep pressure with that locked-out arm. If the arm is locked out the blocker can't get back into me.

The blocker can still try to reach me, but if I am still locked out I can Swim it, or we may Rip it. It is a progression. We do the drill with the blocker leaning into the defender. We lock out and keep the elbow locked. Now we execute the Rip. He should push off on the Rip move. You come back and repeat the drill. If the defender bends his elbow you are going to know it because you are standing behind him. If he bends his elbow the blocker can get back into him. As he comes off the block he makes his Rip move.

When we are teaching the Swim it is the same. The man is locked out and I call out, "Swim it." He pushes up and his move is up and over on the Swim. Those are two escapes that we use. We lock out and Rip. We clear the hips, and then we work up to the Swim. We lock out, clear the hips, and then Swim.

The first progression is to get the blocker just standing there. We are not doing anything, he is just standing there. One of the things I do is to line them all up across from each other. I tell them to do their progression. I suggest you get behind them so you can see their elbows.

Next we go to the escape down the line. Now I put them literally on the line. I put the defensive man's feet on the line of scrimmage. I put an offensive man straight across from him. We have just taught them how to escape. Initially we are not escaping. We are just working down the line. We pair them up and start working. We work our hips. A key point is to get a quick shuffle step. As you start down the line you want to shuffle with a vertical push. We are fitted up with the blocker. You can tell what kind of a vertical push he is getting because he is on the line. We want to move our feet into the neutral zone if we can. Then we want to start working down the line.

Next we do the same progression with a back in the drill. We are doing the same thing down the line. You have a defender going against a blocker and running back. The blocker comes off to reach the man. He wants to get a vertical push down the line of scrimmage. Initially we want the running back to run a nice easy course to the outside. The running back stays outside and the defensive man has to escape the block. We tell him to give us a Swim move or a Rip move. We teach them how to get off the block with the running back in the drill. It is vertical push and keep the shoulders square.

Next is the cutback drill. Now we find out how good the defender is. He starts stringing the play out. The running back starts outside and then all of a sudden he cuts back. The defensive man must be able to drop step and pursue the ball late as it crosses the line of scrimmage. If he comes back too soon, the back can bounce. We want him to secure his gap first. This drill teaches the defenders to be patient reading blocks from the outside. We teach them to work outside and then we teach them to work inside.

The last thing in this progression is to use the escape down the line and now we are going to use explode down the line. In explode down the line we have a blocker paired up with the defender. The offensive man talks to his partner on the drill. They are squared off and ready to go. The blocker comes off and engages. We punch step and get ready to get off the block. We are going full speed but we want to use progression teaching. We lock them up first and then we teach them what a Swim move is and what a Rip move is. We find out what they can do well. Some kids are better at one than the other. If we get a short guy we Rip with him. After we get the move we work it down the line. We tell them to escape down the line or to explode down the line.

Next we work on Takeoffs. I use a ball on a stick for this. I know some people have a ball on a string, and some people get down and move the ball with their hand. I get a ball and put it on a broomstick and I can stand there and see everyone. I may have the graduate assistant simulate the snap. We work on takeoffs every day. We line them up four across. We are coming off the ball for five times. We can do any kind of angles or slanting moves. We may call them back one more time and tell them to run one more takeoff just to get them loose. You can work all our moves off the takeoff drill. We move on movement. We key the ball and move on the man across from us.

Now it comes down to Bread and Butter. Before, we were just getting them warm. Now, we are going to get into some true Reads. I like to do a lot of one-on-one reads because that is what it comes down to. It is easy to coach. I coach all the front four. This is how I work them. I want to see how they are doing so I line them all across a line. I may have eight, 10, or 12 players paired off. I will stand behind the defense. I give a direction for the offense to block the man.

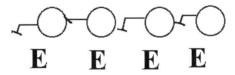

E   E   E   E

COACH

We are going to work on the Reach Block or the Scoop Block. We can do a lot on the one-on-one approach. We can incorporate the pass rush, draw reads, and screen reads or what you want to work on. You can work a lot of players in this drill.

Next we go to our Two-on-One Reads. We will do one segment at a time. We will start with the 7 technique on a tight end. It could be a 2 "I" with the tackle. We start with the Reach Block. We are all doing the same techniques. We can have two or three groups working at the same time on the drill. You can work on splits and other things during the drill. You can vary the splits.

We work against the Reach Block. Also, we work on the Scoop Block. We work on the Tackle Guard Scheme and some type of Power Scheme.

We are going to teach the one-on-one drill, the two-on-one, and we are going to do half-line drills. Every day we are going to do some type of group drill against our good people. Also we do our full-line drills.

We use a Circle Drill with our linemen. We line them up behind a cone and have them run inside the circle, and then they go around the outside and go all the way around the circle and finish past the second cone. One thing the drill teaches you is how to bend. It is a good drill to teach leaning and bending. They want to run the circles as tight as they can to the inside. When we talk about a defensive end we are talking about him bending and getting down the line of scrimmage. It is no difference in pass rush. We try to beat a tackle on the outside and bend into the quarterback.

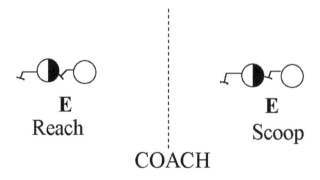

E
Reach

E
Scoop

COACH

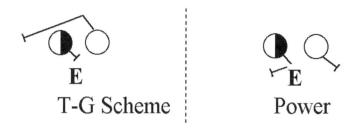

T-G Scheme   Power

COACH

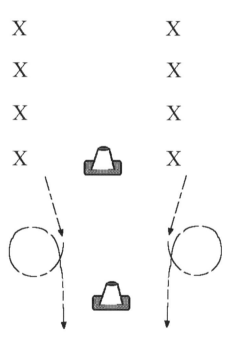

We do all kinds of drills such as Figure Eight. We run a half-circle drill with a cone at one point and the player runs to a second cone in a half circle. It is like the top of the key in basketball. Everyone has to learn how to bend.

Chapter 9

PASS-RUSH TECHNIQUES

Greg Mattison
University of Michigan
1996

I believe rushing the passer is an art and it is a technique. Since I came to Michigan four years ago we have stressed Pass Rush. I think I was taught this lesson at Texas A&M. It is believed the Pass Rush can change the outcome of the game, and the Pass Rush is an art. It is just like anything else you teach—you have to put your time into it.

The first thing to do when looking at your pass rush is to evaluate what you are doing at the present on pass rush. There are a number of ways you can evaluate your pass rush. First is how many sacks you get. That is one of the concrete things you get. It is like the offense. If you are talking about rushing offense, you count the number of rushing touchdowns you score. Sacks to us are very important. We sell the fact to our kids that the ultimate goal when a team is trying to throw the football is to get a sack. We talk to our kids just like you would talk to young kids. We make a big deal about sacks. This year we got 43 sacks. That is the most we have had in years.

The other thing in evaluating your pass rush techniques is to count the number of "pressures" you get. We keep a Production Chart that shows what we are doing in this area each week. Too many times when a guy gets a sack, it is a sack or it isn't. It is not just a black or white situation. Sometimes he will get to the quarterback and force him to hurry his throw. The players have to know they are being rewarded for that pass rush. We sell to our players that we want them to continue the rush up until it is almost late. We don't want a dumb penalty, but anytime we can, we want to let the quarterback know we are getting close to making a sack on him.

The next thing in evaluating the pass rush is to count the number of holding calls against the offense. If it were not for the holding calls, we would have had more sacks. When that happens the player needs to be rewarded. That 15-yard penalty is just as important as a sack. Now, you cannot use the excuse that "he is holding me, coach." Don't buy into that one. When a kid tells me that the blocker is holding him, this is what I tell him: "If someone walks into your house and steals your wallet, what are you going to do about it." Don't let the kids make excuses. Most offensive linemen are Communist anyway. They are taught to hold. That is a part of football. Do not let the kids complain about being held.

When you are evaluating the pass rush, make sure you determine if the team is a running team or not. If a team is only going to throw the ball six or seven times a game, don't expect to get that many sacks. We had an interesting stat this past year. We won nine games. Anytime we got more than two sacks, we won. Three out of the four games, when we got two sacks or less, we lost. That tells you how important the sack is. The sack total really affects the outcome of a game.

The other thing you must consider when evaluating the pass rush is to consider the Sprint-Out Pass. When I talk about the pass rush I like to consider it in several ways. First is the most overlooked phase of the pass rush. This is intelligence. Most every coach gives kids scouting reports. It is no different at Michigan than anywhere else. The importance of the scouting report depends on how big it is. First, you have to have a picture of a defensive lineman. All they want to do is to hit people and make tackles. They could care less about the scouting report if it is one inch thick. What you have to do with the linemen is to accentuate what I call the "Meat." Give them only the things that really mean something to that player. The intelligence factor is that he has to buy into the scouting report. "Hey, when they are in this formation, it is 80 percent pass."

Today, the down linemen need to know the formation. I expect our down linemen to know what formation they are facing. For example, against the One-Back Set it may be 75 percent pass. When our down linemen look at the formation and see it is against a One-Back Set, they had better use that to their advantage. When we get tendencies we are willing to gamble. We want our kids to believe tendencies. If I tell them they should expect a pass from a certain formation, they should really turn loose and go all out.

The other thing we want our linemen aware of is the Backfield Set. In our league, Backfield Sets are correlated to the run and pass. They must get set for that.

Down and Distance is the other thing the linemen must be aware of. If you ask your players what the down and distance is in a game, I would bet you that the down linemen would be the first that do not know. If it is third and 7 and you have that listed as a passing situation, then the down linemen should be down and ready for a street fight. They should be as jacked as they have ever been if they like to rush the passer and they know it is green-light time. It is time to get after that quarterback. Down and Distance is very important. In practice at times, when we are scripting and we are going through a team period, we call out the Down and Distance. Now, it means something to them. If we tell them it is third and 7, I hope the down linemen are using a pass rush technique. If they do run the football against us, that is what we have to practice. You do not want to always practice things that just make your kids look good. We want to give them hard things they will be seeing in a game.

The other thing a lineman must do is to be a scrambler. This really affects how you can rush a passer. I think you have to let the defender to the field and the defender to the boundary, who is your contain man, have a two-way go. If you are not building in the ability, either by stunt or by belief, that he will do the right thing in certain situations to have a two-way go, then you are really hurting that man. The offensive lineman knows if that man is the contain rush man a lot of times. If you do not give him an opportunity to rush inside when he is the outside rush man, then he is not going to be as effective. Don't expect him to be productive in passing situations.

We will talk about offensive players and determine if they are very mobile or not. Our contain man must keep in his rush lane. He has to stay where he can contain against that type of player. If he goes inside and gets beat in that situation, then shame on him.

Next is the use of Film Study. In every game we played this year, there was one out of the five linemen who gave away the pass. There is no doubt about this. We meet with our players and look at the film together. By Wednesday they have to come to us and tell us which lineman is giving away the run or the pass. This helps them in watching film. Defensive linemen may not be the smartest people in the world, and they may not know how to watch the film like others do. You have to teach them how to watch films. If you will tell them to find out who gives the play away, they will look at the films in a different way. When they see us they say, "Coach we got it now." I tell them to let me see the film again to see if they are right.

Another way to do this is to do it in a meeting with them. When you are watching the film, ask them to call out run or pass before each play. You can ask each individual on each play. You should talk to them about Down and Distance when you are watching the film. "What does the scouting report say about third and 7?" This type of exchange has a big influence on them.

The other thing we are concerned about is Splits. It drives me crazy to see this happen to our kids. All of a sudden they read pass and suddenly they have huge splits. How many running plays, when they sit back, are they going to have huge splits? On the other side, when they are closed down tight and you read pass, you know that is a pass. Let the split of the linemen tell you what they are doing. If they have been playing with normal splits and then all of a sudden they close down, it is because they do not want you to get an inside rush.

All of us spend a lot of time in stopping the run. We do the same thing at Michigan. Your character of your defense is tested in stopping the run. But the thing that happens is that you spend a lot of time on a lot of different schemes. Then all of a sudden you start working on the pass rush and you spend all of your time against that one scheme. Now, the offense has different pass protection blocking schemes just as they do for different running plays. It is important for the defensive lineman to know how he is going to be blocked. For example, turn-back protection. How many in here practice against turn-back protection? How many of you practice it in your individual drills? If you are doing it, you are ahead of the game. If you are not and you are going against the drop-back pass, they will get turned back all of the time. They are going to get aggressive blocking all of the time. Working against those blocks is just as important as working against the run block.

The other point is how you are blocked. "The man you are over, John, how does he block you? Is he a retreater? Is he soft? Is he a man that fires out?" That player should be able to give you a scouting report by Thursday. By Wednesday he should be able to tell you the move he is going to use against that offensive player. The man that he goes against is not going to block any differently. He will not change his blocking techniques. You should work your players all week against the individual type of blocks they are going to see in the game. Give him a chance to be a good pass rusher.

The next phase we talk about is the physical phase. This is where we get into what we do differently on defense. When I first came to

Michigan, they were a 5-2 Gap, read-oriented defense, which was a great defense for the run. If I knew you could play both types of defense, I would play 5-2 Gap until the cows came home against the run. That is because you have such a great flat wall. Add the angle slant to that, and you have a tremendous defense. It is a great run defense. The worst defense to rush the passer from is the slant defense. In the slant you are going away from the quarterback. You are not getting into the offense as quickly as you could be. On the 50 defense, you have to sit back and be able to read. As a result you are not a good pass-rush team.

When I got to Michigan we played the 50. But on passing situations, I told them to go to a different stance. The first thing our guys do is adjust their stance when they know it is going to be a pass. We feel the best pass stance is a 3½-point stance. If you are a four-point stance player you are going to be slower. You cannot do the things you have to do in the pass rush, so the three-point stance is the first thing. The next thing we tell them is to get any foot back that they want. If they are right-handed, we want them in a right-hand stance. If they are left-handed, we tell them to get into a left-hand stance. "You get in the best takeoff position you can get in." You have already said it was going to be a pass. You know that third and 8 is a pass situation. He has shown you the pass stance, so get in the best pass-rush stance.

Next we talk to them about narrowing their stance. The most important thing about pass rush is to get to the man as quickly as possible. We want to close the cushion. Most pass rushes are successful or unsuccessful based on how long it takes to get to the man who is blocking them. For the man that is too wide, the first thing that he does is to bring his foot inside. On the first step he has to move his feet closer together and he is not gaining any distance to his man. You want them to spread their feet, but you do not want them to stagger their feet. Young kids see pro players with one foot set way back. It takes that player a long time to get that back foot up where he can attack. As a pass rusher we want to narrow our stance and have almost a toe-to-instep stagger. On that first step I want to gain distance as long and as far as I can, with power. I must be able to get distance forward fast. As soon as I get my foot in the ground and still gain distance, then that is the correct step.

If the man lifts that down hand, he is going to fall on his face. It should look almost uncomfortable. You want to get the butt up in the air so you are coming off the football as hard as you can. To me the stance is the most important thing. It is just like it is in run blocking, and it has to change. You have to get them into a great stance.

The next thing we talk with our men about is rush lanes. Here is where teams are distorted. It is hard to be a disciplined coach and still get this across to your kids. You really have to sell this idea to your kids. Your pass-rush lane is a set gap only until the draw is not there; only until you clear the draw. It drives me crazy for a player to keep running after the quarterback and there are 6 yards between him and the quarterback throwing the ball. He is worried about the draw. "Coach, I have the B Gap rush lane." I tell them this: "You moved your rush lane over to the C and D rush lane." Your rush lane is only a certain gap until there is not a draw. As soon as it is obvious that the draw is not there, you have a straight line to the quarterback. If you want to have success in rushing the passer, your players must know this. Now, if the offense runs the draw in the B Gap and your man runs past the ball, then you have to talk with him. You have to teach him that he has the responsibility to start out with, and if it is there he must make the play. When pass shows, he has a straight line to the quarterback.

The last phase I will talk about before I get into our techniques is our Mental Phase. For your kids to be successful rushing the passer, they must have an unbelievable desire or belief that they can never be blocked one-on-one. The people who make the most in the pros are the great pass rushers. The next highest paid players are the pass blockers. Offensive players get cut going to the pros because they can't pass block quicker than any other reason. You have to put it into the players' terms so they understand what you are telling them. It is ridiculous to think offensive players can pass block the defender one-on-one without holding. Kids must understand you should have the advantage on defense. "It is a sin to get blocked one-on-one on the pass rush? Aren't you letting the team down if you let the man block you one-on-one?"

We go live with our one-on-one each Tuesday and Wednesday. I will guarantee you that we beat the crap out of first-round draft choices all of the time. Every time that kid knows it is a pass in the game, he should go just as he does in that pass drill in practice. That is the attitude he must have. They must strive to never be blocked one-on-one. When we grade film and a player gets blocked in a true passing situation, it is a double minus. It means a lot more when he gets blocked one-on-one and he does not know it is a passing situation. He has to know he is letting the team down. The secondary coaches get their butts ripped if someone gets beat on the long pass and it is not really their fault. The pass coverage is totally correlated with the pass rush.

When we go one-on-one with the offense in practice we always have a big blue bag back deep with a ball hanging on it. More sacks are lost because the rusher does not finish the move. To me the most important part of the pass rush after you get into the blocker is accelerating to the quarterback. When you are doing drills going against the bag, you have to get the rushers to finish. We take it one step beyond making the hit. We want to knock the ball loose. We have the ball tied around the dummy, and it has an elastic rope on the ball. Every time a man comes after the quarterback they are trying to knock the ball on the ground. You must give your players a chance to go for the ball.

The other thing you must sell your team on when you play a passing team is Rotation. If we are playing against a team that throws the ball almost every down, we want to play several players. We will play several players against those teams that like to throw every down. We will play some players that are not as good as the starters. All you ask a player to do is to go as hard as he can when he gets in the game and goes against the pass blocker. We tell them if they will go hard for four plays, we will get them out of the game. You have to sell those subs that you only want four hard plays from them. Then when the next players go in they have to go hard for four plays. When we get into passing situations I believe in substitutions. The players will take pride in those passing situations. We really work hard on the rotation against a passing team.

Now I want to demonstrate the techniques. The first technique we talk about when we are talking about the rush is the Bull Rush. Now, this is the least-used technique. It is the first technique that we teach. It is the rush I want our players to use on the first pass rush of the game. I want them to see if they can knock the blocker on his back on the first pass. What we are going to do is to set this man up. Think about this when you are teaching the pass rush. You do not teach a wrestler 10 moves to master. He can't get good at all of them. You show the wrestler a certain move and tell him to do it perfectly and the only way a player can beat you is to cheat. You are going to counter him on everything he does. So we want to teach one or two great moves and a counter off each of those moves.

The first rush for us is the Bull Rush. The key on this rush is a number of things. First, never reach for the man; punch for the man. It is a three-point punch. If you have defenders that will not put their face into the man, they will not be good pass rushers. I do not think they can be good against run blockers either. When I evaluate prospects, as a defensive line coach that is the first thing I look for. I look for a man who puts his face in there. If he put his face in there, he has a great chance.

When we come out of our stance we talk about closing the cushion. When the blocker sets to pass, I make my move. The first thing I try to do is to explode the heels of my hands and look the chin in. I never tell him to hit with the face because of all of the lawyers out there. So what I do is tell him to look the chin in. It has to be a simultaneous three-point hit. He must be strong enough to take contact with three points and look the chin in and fight them off with the heels of their hands. You will have a chance to have a good Bull Rush. When you grade them on the pass rush, if you can see the player's helmet, then he is wrong. If his helmet is taller than the helmet he is going against, he is wrong. I do not have to evaluate the results. All I have to do is to tell him his helmet is higher than the blocker's helmet. He is too high. You must be pad to pad to have a good Bull Rush.

What we are doing on the Bull Rush the first play of the game is to let the blocker know that we are going to hit him right in the face as hard as we can. The next time it is pass rush, the blocker will brace himself. When an offensive lineman braces himself, he stops moving his feet. Now we have him. We never want to go down the middle of the man. Make sure you understand that. When it is a pass situation, we always want to work on one third of the man. We never want to stay down the middle. If you do that you will lose all day. By the end of the game you will be beat working against those big linemen. Always work on one third of the man. As we make three-point contact on the man, we want to drive that man, and after I clear the draw, I want to move on a straight line to the quarterback. I could make my move to the inside or the outside. Again, it depends on the type of quarterback you are playing against.

An important thing you tell your players in the pass rush is this: when their feet stop, their hands stop. If either or both stop, they lose. They must keep their hands and feet active. The best thing the defense has going for them legally is the use of their hands. The other thing you have going legally is that the blocker is locked. He can't go anywhere. He is going to take three steps back. So the feet become very important. On the Bull Rush we are going to try to make a simultaneous hit on three points. The heels of the hands are going to hit under the cantilever, and we are going to look our chin in. Another important point is to punch through the blocker and not just to him. We want them just like the karate guys. We want them to chop right through that wood or block. When they strike that blow with the heels of the hands they should come up through the man. The most important thing in the Bull Rush is to make the helmet of the blocker go back. If you can get the helmet to pop back, you win. If the helmet does not move, you lose. You have to make the helmet go back and that is why it is a three-point hit.

We drill this with each other in practice. We pair them up across from each other. You have to coach them how to be a good dummy for the drills. The blocker must get on his knees and put his chest down and put his chin down. The reason he has to put his chin down is that he will get his chin cut if you have two aggressive players going against each other. We make the dummy put his chin down so he is protected with his face mask. He gives you a good target and puts his chin down. He must brace himself. We have the defender step and make contact. The hands and helmet must hit at the same time. As coaches, we can close our eyes and tell if they make the hit simultaneously. We hear bang—bang. "No, your hands hit before the helmet did. Try it again." Then we go again. Bang—bang. "No, the helmet hit first." BANG. You can tell if they hit with all three points at the same time. We are not going to kill the dummy. We are working on timing. They get good at it and then you let them go live. It is BOOM! That helmet jerks back. Now we have a chance.

Another point that will kill your pass rush is this: Don't let go of the jersey. So many times you have a kid that makes a great hit on the first contact, and as he is driving, his hand comes off the blocker's pad. Always teach your kids to punch and grab. When you are running pass-rush drills you should have them striking the blow and then grabbing the blocker's jersey. If you don't, they will just hit and slap instead of grabbing. The Bull Rush is a technique we are going to use against a Three-Step Drop team. All we are trying to do is to knock the blocker back into the quarterback and finish with your hands up in the air. The other thing is it softens the blocker up for the next pass. From the Bull Rush we go to our teaching progression. When we get through all of them, we tie them together.

The reason I am taking so much time going over this technique is this. I get so sick of hearing how the quarterback could practice all year long and all summer without a ball. Now, these guys can become great pass rushers without using a football. All they need is a partner.

The next thing we do is called Butt and Flip. We are going to make three-point contact. On the first rush we make a Bull Rush. The blocker is expecting a Bull Rush on the second rush. He is going to brace for the Bull Rush. Offensive linemen hate to get knocked back into the quarterback. When he gets beat on a sack, the quarterback does not know who has made the sack. When that big blocker is sitting in the quarterback's lap, he gets upset. So the blocker is going to brace.

I was taught a long time ago that when an offensive lineman is blocking he should hang a whistle around his neck. If the blocker is in perfect pass protection position, that whistle will hang right down between his legs. If that whistle comes back against his chest, he has come back too far. If the whistle is out over the blocker's toes, he is overextended. I talk to our defensive linemen about getting the blocker out of the "Whistle Position." We tell them to "Move the Whistle." They know what we are talking about.

We are going to get the man off balance. If he is going to sit back and the whistle is going to go against his chest, we are going to run him right through the quarterback as we work an edge. If you hit the man hard early, they will get the whistle out over their body.

When the man makes a move to keep us from driving him back, that is when we are going to our Flip Technique. We are going to use his bad technique to our advantage. We are going to butt him. As we feel his weight forward, it is a progression for us. If he is leaning on me, I step to the side and pull down at the same time. Remember my face is right under his chin. I just butted him, and his head went back. Now his weight is coming forward with his weight. Now I step to the side and tuck my hips.

We practice the moves on the numbers. I tell the players to get into position. I call out 1 and we get a three-point hit. I call out 2 and we should be stepping to the side and pulling him down at the same time. That is the key point. You are going to get players that make mistakes and he is going to pull the man into his body. You do not do much with the man's arm except let him go where his weight takes him.

When you teach the Flip you should teach it by the numbers. The dummy has to be taught to lean. He has to do like the blocker will do in a game. In breaking down the teaching progression, we eliminate 1. We tell everyone to get into position for 2. Now we work our step-around.

What do we do from this point? We do what we call the Rip. Our favorite move is the Rip. We like the arm Rip. Why? Because it keeps you low. I do not like the arm over that much. For some kids it is fine. I never call it Swim. So we are talking about Rip.

On the mechanics of Rip we forget phase one and two and go to phase three. What is phase three? He has his hands on the man and we are going to Rip. On the Rip Technique it is critical that you always Rip the same arm and leg. We say "Rip Arm and Rip Leg." You must move with the same arm and leg together. You have to sell them on the fact the two are tied together. You can move the leg without moving the arm. All of your strength comes from the hips. We want to step and bring the Rip arm straight up underneath the blocker's armpit. At the same time, the leg is coming through.

The first point is the three-point hit. The second point is to flip the hips. The third point is to step and Rip at the same time. The most important point to remember when you get to the third step is that you must point your toes toward the quarterback. If you do not point your toes to the quarterback, you are beat. If the quarterback is set up in his pocket and your toes go out to the side, you are beat. The quarterback is not over on the side. My rush lane is a straight line to the quarterback. There is no draw. We point our toes at the quarterback and dip the tip of the shoulder and drive. Soon I am by the man. You have to keep your toes pointed toward the quarterback.

How do we break that part of it down? Have everyone get into a Rip position. We go against each other as we did before. It is butt, flip, rip. The only way a man can beat you once you get a Rip position on him, in my opinion, is to cheat. The most common way he cheats is to drive you wide away from the quarterback. When we lock up, he tries to drive us away from the quarterback. Now he becomes a run blocker. The quarterback is inside. If you are worth your salt, he will not push you outside. When he starts driving you outside, this is when you must take advantage of him. Now he is cheating and you have to take advantage of him.

There are three ways we beat this move, or ways we counter the move. This is our first counter. We have the Butt Flip, and now here is the counter off it when the blocker starts driving you. As soon as I feel pressure on the hip and he starts driving and his momentum is driving me away from the quarterback, I grab him and drop step and club behind him. Where is my rush lane? It is a straight line to the quarterback. When I feel him taking me away from the quarterback, I drop my outside foot and drop step and pull him at the same time. He is cheating by being overextended. I pull him forward and club and go around him. If you miss the move, you are back to a restart position.

The first counter is to plant the outside foot, drop step, club, and finish all moves with the Rip. This is true if there is air or a man there.

The other counter is to plant the inside foot and work against the blocker's wrist by turning it over. We roll the thumb down and turn him away. There is no way he can stop me on that. What is the key? Sell the Bull Rush.

The last move that he can stop us with is the Sink Down. When I am ripping him and lifting him, he is sinking. He is cheating because his weight is going down. Use his momentum. Now all I do is roll my butt down and go on over him. We roll his elbow down and move around him. We twist up at the same time.

How do we get all of this taught? We drill this like wrestling. We take what the blocker gives. We put them in position and work with them. We give them different moves to let them get the feel of what we want. It is just like wrestling in that they must feel the moves.

If we have our wishes, we would never want to get tied up with a blocker. If it is third and 7 we do not do a Bull Rush. I do not want a Club and Rip if I do not have to. If it is third and 7 we want to get on the edge of the man and go. We have two ways of getting on the edge. The first move is what we call a Speed Club move. The first thing we do is to widen out more. It is a passing situation. I know the blocker has one thing to do. He can slide to the outside, or he can slide back and then slide to the outside. What is he taught? He can carry 260 pounds. He wants me to run into his body. What do I want to do? I want to get on the edge. We do what we call a Speed Club move. We are doing everything we just talked about except we are not doing it from a Butt Flip. If I am in a left-hand stance I must have my feet up under me on the snap of the ball. I do not want my feet to be spread out. I want a narrow stance. When the blocker flinches or that ball moves, I want to explode and get my hips into the man. BOOM! As soon as I get past the man's hip, I win. I am going to get out of my stance that I got in when I was inside. Now, I am not getting all tied up with that big blocker. You must kick that arm and leg together as you come across. If I am doing what I am supposed to do, I will get to the edge.

We have officials come and work our practices. When I first got there they would tell me my guys were lined up offside. I told them great.

I do not want them doing that in a game, but I want them up on the ball. If the defense expects a pass and he is back off the ball, he is nuts. I want to be almost offside. If you do that, don't bitch at your players for lining up offside in a game.

The next thing is this: What can he do to take away my edge? What are most offensive linemen told? "Never get beat inside." In our scheme of pass rush we go to our Counter Step. All that is to sell the blocker on either an inside move or the Bull Rush. On both of these, the feet should look the same. On the snap of the ball we step real hard down the middle of the blocker. Doing this freezes him. Now I am where I want to be. He did not step outside. I am right back where I want to be. If he does not think I have an inside move, we are where we want to be. The mechanics on a Counter Step are these: One, you cannot take a big step. The worst thing your kids will do when you give a Counter Step is to step inside. It has to be a straight step. You want to widen the linemen, if anything. As soon as we step straight at him, he thinks we are coming inside or we are running the Bull Rush. Now we have the edge on him.

The other mistake your kids will make on the Counter Step is that they do not step like it is a Speed move. When you are using a Speed Club, gain distance. What the kids do on the Counter Step is to take little steps. That will not get them to the edge. When you go to the Speed move, you have to get the hips out and get down in the crotch on them. The Counter Step is always straight ahead from a wider alignment tight to the line of scrimmage with a short first step. If it is a true passing situation, or if your kids have gotten good, you want to do it with a hand flash. You have all three moves from there.

One move that I like is for players who have gotten good at rushing the passer. It is what we call the Speed Spin. I am not a big believer in the Spin, but I am a believer in giving a guy a chance and in giving the rusher a way to get to the quarterback. The Speed Spin incorporates everything you have taught in your defense. It is the Speed Club. If we had a number 1 move, it would be the Speed Club Rip. That is what we are trying to get to every time. All the Spin does is this: You are showing a Club move without touching the man.

On the snap of the football I want to drive the tip of my shoulder into his numbers. Where will his hands go? He feels pressure and he thinks I am doing a Rip move. I drop my hip and make my move from there. One of the ways they stop this move is to retreat. There are a couple of variations you can use. We do not use them much, but we do teach them to the kids.

The last move I will talk about is called the Stab. The Lions did this a couple of years ago, and we picked it up from them. I do not believe we should ever get blocked. I am sure you offensive line coaches can tell that. I know it doesn't happen this easily. I believe no one should ever block the defensive man one-on-one. If you get in a situation when you are out wide and you did not get the edge, what is your recourse? The blocker is quicker than you are and he has beaten you. What are you going to do? He has you now. You can't come back inside because he has you again. We do what we call the Stab. A Stab technique is this: From a locked-up position I have nothing up inside. But if I drop my hand down and come around I am a lot better off. We want to take that free hand and punch him in the sternum as hard as we can and grab. This will keep you from getting locked inside with both hands tied up. It is a great way to keep movement toward the quarterback.

A couple of coaching points. We start off every practice after we do our agilitys with what we call a Free Ball Get Off. There is nothing new on this drill. It tells our players that we want them to get off on the snap of the football. We put a Green Ball down and have them key the ball. The reason we use a green ball is so they will really focus on the ball. It is different. It is something they have to focus on. One of the worst things kids do on pass rush is that they do not focus. It is just like a sprinter. They have to get off as fast as they can. If they see everything and do not see what you should be looking at, you will be slow. You have to focus on what you are going to be teaching your kids. If you have them looking at the ball, they should be looking at one thing.

Another drill we use is great. We take two kids and line them up with a coach in front of them holding a tennis ball. Then the coach lets go of the ball. The players go after the ball. You do not let them dive for the ball. They must move their feet. You can find out who can move on this drill. What does this drill show you? They are so much faster when you drop the tennis ball. Why? Because they are so much more focused. You show the players that they are fast when you drop the tennis ball. Tell them the offensive man's shoulder pad should be the tennis ball. When it moves, he should move. If you want them looking in at the football, it becomes the tennis ball. You tell them if they do not focus, they do not play.

The other thing we do is at the end of practice. The first year I got to Michigan they had 24 sacks the year before. I was in shock coming from Texas A&M. I knew we had to do something about the sacks.

We decided we would do pass rush every day at the end of practice. They finished with what we called "Follow the Leader." You can use anything you want. You can use the sled or you can use a senior or a captain or anyone you want. They come up front and do something different each day. The man is up front and he has eight men behind him. He is going to use the Speed Club move. I move the ball and they make the move. Then the next player makes his move on the ball. We finish up with something like that every day.

The other thing we do is we have a Sack Board. If sacks are important you have to let the entire team know they are important. In our hallway leading down to the meeting room we have a big slate chalkboard. It has all of the teams on our schedule listed down the board. At the end we have the Rose Bowl. When a kid gets a sack, his picture goes on that slate board. Most of the players are interested in this. It gets their attention. Another thing is that it gives you a running total of the number of sacks you have each year. You can see how you are doing each game. It is a real motivating thing as well.

We really do a lot with a Production Chart. It also is a big slate board. Each kid's name is on the slate as a football field. We have 50 yards and then 50 more yards. Every game we grade our kids with a plus or minus on technique. The most important grade we give them is on production. We all have had players that were perfect. He plays everything the way he is supposed to in practice, but he never makes a tackle in the game. He never misses an assignment, but he never makes any big plays. Then you have the player that plays five plays and he makes two sacks and a fumble recovery. Why isn't he in there? "Well, he is not very disciplined." You are going to win more games with that man than you will with the perfect practice player. It is unbelievable what that board will do for the players. We grade them by production yards. We give minus points on missed tackles. Our kids come in and look at the board. We give them a grade with tape on the board to show how many yards their production was for that week. The color of the tape is the color of the team we played against the past game. Against Illinois we had orange tape. Against Boston College we used maroon tape. You can follow the board all the way across the field.

Chapter 10

PASS-RUSH TECHNIQUES

Jim Muehling
Indiana University
1993

I am going to talk about defensive line play with regard to rushing the passer. I will talk about the elements that we use as far as the pass rush, the pass-rush moves, the drills we use, and some of the power moves we teach.

First, I want to talk about our philosophy of rushing the passer. This is dictated by the defense we are playing. We play a couple of different fronts. We play a 4-3 front that is more of an attacking front. We lay our ears back and move on the snap of the ball. It is a ball-key defense. We have an area that we are attacking on the snap of the football. On our nickel front, which is a 4 front, it is a little less aggressive at the snap of the football for the inside people because we are short one linebacker. We have two linebackers instead of three in our nickel front. We slide the fronts some, particularly with a two-back set. We will give them more of a 50 look with a nose man. It is less aggressive than our 4-3 package.

We use two types of pass-rush moves. We use the speed rush and the read-and-react rush. Once you get into the moves, there is no difference in the moves. You start executing the move, and the principles of the moves do not change. The philosophy of your defense will dictate the kinds of moves you want to teach on the pass rush. If you are an attacking-type defense where you want to lay your ears back and come hard, you do not have a lot of reads for the front people. You are going to teach a lot more speeds and rip-and-slip moves, such as the butt and olé moves, which I will cover later.

In our philosophy, we talk about the desire to get to the quarterback. A lot of players are a little tentative at this. If you are going to chew out a kid because of the draw play, you need to make sure you have the right person who is responsible for the draw. It all depends on who you assign the draw to. It is like hitting a golf ball. Do you want me to take a wood and hit it as hard as I can, or do you want me to take an iron and hit it straight down the fairway? It depends on what you want. You have to let the kids know what you want.

You must make time to get better. We spend three periods a day in practice trying to get better on the pass rush. The time will vary on each period, but we do have three periods to teach the pass rush. I think you can do the same with the pass rush in high school. You have to make time to get better. I know that some of you have players that go both ways. Some of you have defensive specialists, and you can get a lot of things down on the pass rush.

We spend five to 10 minutes per day on pass-rush technique. We work on takeoff, ball-key moves, and breaking the corner down. We spend a minimum of 10 minutes on group work every day, defense against the offense. We use a drill we call "machine gun," where we set up cones and have them rush the passer. The tackle goes with a guard; however, the guard is only for alignment. He steps out of the way once the ball is snapped.

We go one-on-one on the pass rush. We go bang, bang, bang! We are just like a machine gun. We go one after another. The coach on offense blows the whistle. We get a lot of three- and four-step pass rushes. We set a ball on top of a dummy at a depth of 5 or 7 yards deep to simulate a quarterback setting up to throw the pass. That is where the tackle is working toward.

We do not like to do a lot of full-line work. We do a lot of half-line work. We do team work later in the practice session. We go 1's versus 1's and 2's versus 2's at the end of practice. While the group work is going on, the skeleton drill is going on at the other end of the field for our linebackers. We incorporate some offensive backs for protection in our drills. Also, we will bring up some linebackers. However, during that drill, it is the front linemen going against each other.

Next, we have team pass period for 10 minutes. We may go 15 minutes, depending on what we have done in the other 15-minute drills. Early in the year, we may not do any team work during practice. Later in the year, we may do more team work and less group work.

Let me get into the principle of the pass rush. We have 10 principles that we cover in our pass-rush package.

Principles of Pass Rush

1. Speed for speed! We spend a lot of time, since we are in the 4-3 front, looking at the football. As soon as the center flinches his hands, we move. Also, we work under the chutes, and we move from a painted line. We make sure that the ball is in the middle of the defense. A coach checks their stance and moves the ball. We make sure that they are getting off on the ball. We work on the takeoff drill every day. It may be for only one minute or for only 30 seconds per day. We come out of our stance and get ready to attack, speed for speed! We want to get the offensive lineman in a disadvantaged position with our speed. We want to take the bend out of his knees where he has to kick out of his alignment. With our speed, we are going to get his weight moving off the center of gravity as much as possible. This puts him at a disadvantage by forcing him to go backward. This is what we mean by speed for speed. We have to teach him to come out of his stance.

    Speed off the read! Many of you in high school may play a read defense. Once you do read pass, speed off the read to rush the passer. We will put them into a position where they are locked up and go from there. We are always using our hands on the rush. We will cover these moves later. We are trying to reach through and get that cloth behind his shoulder pad. We want to pull him forward so we can get by his hip. If you use your hands on the pass rush, you always use the foot on the same side as the hand you use. Do not cross the hands and feet. We stress this coaching point: Step through; step through. Close the distance between the blocker and the quarterback.

2. Constant up-the-field movement, no lateral moves. We constantly tell them to get their butts up the field. We want to close the distance between the quarterback and blocker as quickly as possible.

3. Force the blocker's shoulders to turn; work to the corner. The offense is trying to keep their shoulders square to the line of scrimmage. They are trying to keep their hips square so they can react to the pass rush. They will take away one side or the other. Most of the time, they will try to force us to take the long way outside. On defense, we want to force shoulder turns by applying pressure to one side and pulling the inside shoulder or by getting the outside shoulder turned. That is what we are trying to get. We are trying to get a shoulder turned. We are going to

push it, or we are going to pull it. Let me talk about the hand moves. We are trying to throw speed moves. We do not get both hands on the man, usually. When we do get the hands on the man, we go for the shoulder pads. We shoot our hands for the wide corners of the shoulder pads.

4. Take the bend out of his knees; force the grab. I am trying to get to the blocker as soon as possible. I always keep leverage on the blocker. I want my pads below his shoulder pads. I want to be able to force up and into the blocker, or I can get the force where I can pull down through him to get the bend out of his knees.

   If I get the bend out of the blocker's knees, he cannot move. As soon as his knees get straight, he can't move. This is true on defense as well as on offense. We want to take the bend out of the blocker's knees as quickly as possible. We want to force the grab. We want him to grab for us to save his own rear end from getting beat. We want to force the hold so he will get a flag on the play. We feel that the holding penalty is not called enough, but the offense feels it is called too much. If we can force the hold, the officials will call it every once in a while.

5. Maintain body lean; lead with the hard stuff! Give the blocker as little soft stuff as possible. We want to lead with the shoulders out over the knees. I want to pass-rush with my shoulders out in front of my knees. I do not want to rush straight up. I do not want two chickens fighting. We rush with body lean. They give us this big helmet, face mask, and shoulder pads, so we lead with the hard stuff. Don't give them much of the soft stuff, which is your body. If the blocker is trying to grab you, make him grab the hard stuff and not the soft stuff. This is the reason that we tell them they are too high. They must have body lean.

6. Maintain a power position. Keep your shoulders lower than the blocker. (Kick off if necessary.) What is a power position? You are getting ready to clean the blocker. You are going to power-clean the blocker.

7. Force the retreat; don't let the quarterback set his feet. We know that you are not always going to get to the quarterback. We would like to change his rhythm and the tempo of the throw. That is one of the things that we keep track of on our production points. We give awards for our sacks. We can't just pat them on the back. We award them for tips, forced bad passes, and other good plays.

8. No recoil off blocks! Keep pressure hard, fast, and constant. We are going north and south on our pass rush. Keep the pressure up the field and not lateral.

9. Work to get on the same yard line as the blocker. If you do, he's beat! (Pressure back into the quarterback.) We want to get on the same yard line as the blocker. If we can do that, we have him beat. If we can look him in the ear hole, he is beaten. We try to get to the point—to the tip of his shoulder or the tip of his hip.

10. Stay on the ground until throwing motion starts, skywalk, hands high (tip drill). How many times have you seen the rusher leap up in the air to block a pass, and then the quarterback ducks under him and makes a big play? We run a drill to work on this technique. We want to keep the feet on the ground and keep up the field until the throwing motion starts. When the throwing elbow goes up, that is when we will stop and get our hands up in the air. On the release of the ball, we are jumping and tipping. In the drill, we have them call out "pass" when the quarterback makes his drop. When the off arm comes off the ball, we call "ball." This is to let the defensive back know that the ball is ready to be released. The scout-team quarterback throws a volleyball-type pass so the rushers can practice tipping the ball. They can knock it down or reject it. If they catch the batted ball, they can run with it. They have a lot of fun with the drill.

Pass-Rush Lanes

On our field, we use the dome-shaped pass-rush lanes; we have a five-step and a seven-step lane. We have the lanes drawn on our grass field, and we use them in our machine-gun drill.

1. Simple points of aim (near number, near shoulder)

2. Lines on practice field for drop-back

3. Drill work with a "rabbit" for one half roll and sprint

4. Give the rusher some freedom to do it.

5. Understand how blitz affects lanes T's in A/E's contain (or E's/under).

Types of Pass-Rush and Rush Moves Read Rush

Let's say you are in a 50 defense. You have a 5 technique, a 4 technique, a 6-technique end, and a nose man. You have an end coming off the back side. You have a four-man rush coming off the read. You are reacting off that read to execute the pass-rush move.

1. Define—First I play run, and then I read pass. Now I have to execute my pass-rush move. That is a read pass rush.

2. Principles—On the read rush, we use the following points.

   a. Three-point explosion—Arm extension, take the bend out of his knees, and I can get his shoulders raised. The hands are two points; the face looking in is the third point.

   b. Power position—You must have power position on the blocker when you use a read rush. You must be able to get him up in the air, and you must be able to get your shoulders underneath him. We work off the push and the pull.

   c. Take away the knee bend.

3. Lift and rip, jerk and slip—These are the basic two moves that we use. We call it the slip because Coach Mallory does not want to call it a swim move. It rhymes with *rip,* and we are not going to swim at Indiana. Coach Mallory hates the term *swim.*

Speed Rush

1. Define—We are a ball-key team. When the ball moves, we attack. That is a speed rush. If it is a run, I must adjust as I attack the line of scrimmage. If it is a pass, I must execute a pass-rush move on the run. That is a speed rush.

2. Principles

   a. Elongated step

   b. Cloth grab

   c. Breakdown

   d. Move execution

3. Get to the corner!

Pass-Rush Moves (Read and Speed)

(Both) indicates that you can use on read and speed rush.

1. Rip (both)—At this time of the year, this is what we do in the weight room. We take weights or plates, because we do not have enough dumbbells. We use a drill we call 10 o'clock–2 o'clock. We take the weights in our palms and try to get the arms extended to 2 and 10 o'clock on the face of a clock. We want to get the arm under the man and drive it up through the man. They do three sets of eight reps. That is the way we work on the rip. The

key point on the rip is to stay as close to the blocker's body as possible, stepping on the back of his heel on the back side.

2. Slip (both) — You want to make it as tight to his body as possible. Again, on the read rush, this is off a pull on the low shoulder, or it is off the near shoulder on the speed rush. We are trying to rub paint with his body. We are going to be tight on the man.

3. Bull (read) — If we get a man off balance so he can't get back on a power position, we will run him back to the quarterback. We will try to make the tackle with the blocker. It is a bull rush. We want to turn loose and go all out.

4. Olé (read) — This is a move of the bull-rush move. It is a read situation. We are trying to take the momentum that the man is giving us and use it to get by him. We want to throw our elbow into our body tightly, spin on our foot, and pull him around. We want to pull the elbow into our body, so we have separation with him, and then redirect. We will finish with a rip move on the back side.

5. Swat and hop (both) — This is a move we got from the Raiders. It is similar to the olé move. They are making a swat with the hand and a hop on the move. They are hopping into the line of scrimmage and going with an arm rip to the quarterback. It is a good speed move. Most kids can execute it without any problems. You can install this when they are in shorts and T-shirts.

I have given you five moves. Most players will only use one or two moves. We do not practice some moves for some players.

Next, I want to discuss some countermoves for the read and speed rush. We have a "Reggie" move that we got from Reggie White of the Eagles. That is when you are stuck on a rip move. The off hand is very important. We want to take his momentum in the direction that he is taking us. I withdraw the rip move, get the inside hand on his hip, and widen the rush lane. It is a countermove off the rip move.

The "whirling dervish" is a spin move. I do not like the spin moves because you lose sight of the quarterback. Most of the time, you give back the ground that you have already won when you spin. Some players can do it well. A lot of kids will spin back one way or the other naturally. If they are stuck on a rip move, they want to come back on a spin move. They want to sink the butt as quick as possible. They want to get the backside leg into the line of scrimmage as quickly as they can and as far as they can.

I want to quickly cover a couple of escape moves that we teach. The biggest thing we like to counteract is the arm clamp. We use the limp-arm slip. I will just call it "limp-arm over." Don't fight it any more, turn it limp, and then go to the slip on the back side. I like to use the rip move. Also, we like to use the lift-off move and the under/over moves.

Quick Hands

We use some drills with our hands. It is all of that kung fu stuff. All I am trying to do is to teach them to use their hands. They work well on the speed move. This is what we do against hands extended.

1. Double club over—The blocker has his hands extended. We take the hands, go over the blocker's hands, and break his shoulders down. You have to get the hands to a slip move.

2. Double club under—This is the same thing. Now, we bring the hands underneath the blocker's extended hands. Then we do our rip move.

3. Side club (left or right)—We club to the right or left side. We must step to the side we use the club on.

4. Cross club (left or right)—This is a cross-over-the-body move. We cross over and step through. It is good move on the perimeter.

I want to close with some ideas on motivation. We have a slogan that we use to remind us that we need to motivate our players: "Push 'em, but pull 'em, too!" We give weekly awards and seasonal awards.

Motivation

1. Get to the passer—Each week we have a "get-to-the-passer" award. Also, we give this award to someone at the end of the year. It is a big deal for us.

2. 50-sack board—We have a board that we use to keep track of the sacks. Our goal is to get 50 sacks. We keep this up to date and go over it every Monday in our meeting. It is a team award.

3. Point systems (pressure pays)—We keep individual awards for the end of the year. There are some things you can do to reward the players. We get most of our information from the film.

Point System

A. Sacks

B. Hurries

C. Pull-downs

D. Flushes

E. Tipped balls

F. Caused interception

G. Making a pass or run = no first down

H. Caused a penalty (hold, clip, face mask, etc.)

We give them a point value for each of the goals. We value each of these goals before the start of the season. We assign one, two, or three points for each of the good plays. They can lose points if they make a bad play.

Chapter 11

OVERVIEW OF THE KENTUCKY DEFENSE

Larry New
University of Kentucky
1991

I want to share our defensive philosophy with you and talk about our defense. It is totally impossible for me to give you everything we do in our defensive system at the University of Kentucky in 90 minutes.

Actually the game is a lot simpler than a lot of us make it when we get up to lecture. I do not come to clinics to try to pick up a new offensive or defensive scheme. I come to a clinic and listen to the speakers looking for the little things than I might be able to use in our techniques or in our schemes. I am not here to sell our system. If I can give you a couple of things that will help you organize your defensive scheme, or help you develop a defensive scheme or package, and give you a couple of things that will help you coach the defense better, or communicate better on defense, then I will have accomplished what I came here to do.

I do not think there is any difference in what we are doing and what others are doing. Defenses in major colleges today are Multiple. There are very few people in college football that line up in one defense and in one coverage and play that same defense and same coverage all day. In my experiences I have found that if you line up in one defense and play only one coverage all day, you had better be a lot better than your opponent or they are going to kick the living daylights out of you. It is that simple. They will line up and scheme you. Defenses have become multiple because the offense has become so complicated. We have to know every formation, who is in the game, and all of the other aspects of the offense. I would love to see the offense go back to the days of 1950s football.

There is a tremendous amount of strategy to the game today. There is a tremendous amount of multiplicity to the game. Today in football you can get your butt beat before the ball is snapped if you do not adjust to the offense. You had better line up right and adjust right, or they will have you outnumbered and flanked. They line up and run motion, they will get into Trips and No-Backs and One-Back and run Shotgun and everything in the books. You have to be able to adjust. When we started putting our defensive scheme together we started looking at some of those things. If we line up a tackle in a 3 technique and we play him there all day, I assure they will block that 3 technique man if you leave him there all night. I do not care if he is Godzilla Jr., they will find a blocking scheme to block him. There is not a technique that will take care of everything on defense. They have all the answers to what you do on defense. What they don't like is for the defense to be in a different look where they can't determine what the defense is going to do. That gives the offense problems, and that is why we are multiple on defense.

What is Multiple? Multiple is more than Two; it is not more than 5,000. That is all multiple is; more than two. The key to multiplicity is more than two defenses and being able to execute the defense and play them. That is what multiple is to us. Some people are multiple with three or four fronts. Some are multiple with 40 fronts. It doesn't make any difference, the important thing is being able to communicate them, first, and then execute the defenses. If they can do this you are multiple. How multiple you become depends on how much your players can handle. I have seen teams go to a Multiple Defense over the years. They build one phase of the defense at a time until they get what they want. By the end of the year they have a defensive package. They do not build it overnight. After a two- or three-year period they have a lot of defensive schemes. They do it in segments.

A lot of our multiplicity came about in our package. We have a package of things that we do on defense. Bill Glaser, who coaches our down linemen, joined us from Jerry Claiborne's staff when we came to Kentucky. When we started putting in our Multiple Defense Bill said, "This defense is like a nuclear reactor." There is just no end to this defense. Our defense lends itself to creativity. I want to give the offense a new bastard

every week. It is not new to our kids because it is built into our system. It will be something our opponents have never seen from us. We will run something that is totally new to them. This is a nightmare for offenses. They call us multiple in a lot of ways. Let me tell you this about multiple fronts: If we move a man six inches, that becomes a new front. This amazes me. We can move a man six inches and the offense wants to take a time-out and talk things over. They want to take 30 minutes on the bags to figure out how to block the changes we made and we only moved a man from a 3 technique to a 4 technique. We move a man six inches and they think we are trying to screw them again. If six inches here and six inches there can give them that much problem then we want to be multiple.

I like a lot of defenses. Each defense gives you something another one doesn't. We have used the 4-3, 5-2, Eagle, 6-1, Split, Wide Tackle, and a lot of others. We play a lot of these fronts because we want to take advantage of the best features of each defense. Doing this allows us to give the offense some problems. We are not going to give each defense a different name; we are going to build our defense within our system. If you are going to be a good coach on defense you must study the offense. I spend a lot of my time at a clinic like this listening to speakers talk about the offense. I want to know what the offensive people are teaching so I will know how to beat them. If you are going to play great defense up front you have to beat blocking schemes. You can do it with multiplicity and you can do it by stemming, you can do it by stunting, and you can do it by playing straight technique. You have to have a game plan to beat blocking schemes. No longer is the game "the best man wins." If you go back home and get out the game films you will see that most football today is nothing more than Wing-T football out of the I-Formation and a lot of different sets. I have not seen a Base Block in so long, I can't remember when it was done last. There is no Base Blocking anymore. Not many teams come off the ball and come straight at the defense and try to knock you off the football. Oh, I see inside cutoff, and I see reach, and I see zone blocks, and a lot of other similar blocks. But I do not see any Base Blocking today; it is all angle blocking now.

In order to build the defense and to have a philosophy on defense, you must understand the offense. You have to counteract the offense. The first thing you must do is to build around your personnel. This is where multiplicity helps us. If you only have one defensive scheme and your personnel cannot play it, then you are just out of luck. I have a hard time trying to coach with people that are not suited for a certain defense. I get tired of telling them to "get lower, get tougher, get mean out there." That doesn't get the job done on defense. The offense is moving the ball down the field and we are sitting there in the same defense yelling, "Get down." This is what we have to do. We either put in another player in that hole, or we go to another defense. They are getting ready to score and we must adjust to what they are doing to us. I have been through the old method of telling the players it will get better and in the third quarter they are still pounding the ball down our throat. I want to give our defense something we can adjust to that will help us play better. Give the defense something else that will help them. If you only have one front, you can't help him very much. This is the only solution. *It is our jobs as coaches to give our players a chance to win.* Do you understand that?

If the offense is kicking our tackle's ass, give him a chance to win by changing up the defense. Don't sit around after the game and blame the kids. If they are running through the off-tackle hole, run two or three men in there to stop them. But stop them! Don't just sit there and let them keep running off tackle. Then, when the game is over you say, "They just kicked our butts." At least make them run the other way. Don't give the offense a lot of credit. I have moved four players in a gap to stop the off-tackle play. We move players around on defense to stop a play and think we are going to get killed somewhere else. I have done this and the offense will still run the ball into four men in the off-tackle hole. They only change plays about half of the time. They get lucky at times, I know that. A blind hog finds an acorn every now and then if he scratches long enough. Don't give them too much credit on offense.

Multiplicity allows you to build around your personnel. If you have a team that has a lot of linebacker personnel, then you should be in a defense that utilizes a lot of linebackers. If you have a lot of good linemen then you should be multiple enough to get into that defense. If you have a great player, then utilize him. Give yourself a chance with your defense for that player to be a dominating player. Move him around. Put him in a lot of positions where the offense will have to figure out where he is lined up. If you have a great player, don't line him up in the same place every down. If you do that the offense will line up and run away from him. Move him around and make the offense figure out where he will line up next. We utilize our personnel.

This is a list of things we feel the offense wants to do against our defense. This is what we look at against the offense:

A. Mismatch

B. Predictability

C. Simplicity (Base Defense)

D. Cause confusion

E. Soft on perimeter support

F. Little or no pressure

G. To be methodical

H. To be rhythmical

We want to create a Mismatch on defense. That is where I am involved as the Defensive Coordinator. I want to create mismatches. How do you create a mismatch? You have to evaluate the offensive personnel. Don't try to mismatch against Godzilla Jr. Get the mismatch against Pee Wee Jr. That is where you want to work on the mismatch. Some coaches will say they want to run at the biggest, fastest, and toughest man on defense. Then if they can beat him they can whip the entire defense. But, if they can't whip the best man by running right at him, they are not going to win the battle. I do not want to create my mismatch on their best player. I want the mismatches against the weak players. I want to isolate their weak players and make them play one-on-one. In that mismatch, we win. If we get the one-on-one mismatch with their best player, we are not going to win that battle.

Another thing the offense is looking for is Simplicity. When you go to a clinic what defense does the offensive coaches draw their plays up against? Have you ever seen someone talk on offense and talk about blocking anything except the 5-4 defense when he give his lecture? They can really block the hell out of that defense. They can butcher the hell out of that defense. This is what they want, simplicity. If you line up on defense and only give them one thing, they love it. If they love simplicity, then we need to give them multiplicity. That is a good reason for a Multiple Defense.

Another thing the offense wants to do is to soften your perimeter support. As you build the defensive scheme you must make sure you have your perimeter set. You must have the ability to adjust your perimeter defense. The ability to keep your primary support set if possible is important against motion and shifting. If you can adjust your defense without changing your primary support, you are better off. There are times when you can't do that. But if you can, it is much better. The offense wants to take a tiny 135-pound wide-out and bring him back across the formation wanting you to change your defensive coverage and primary support. Half of the time, that little piss ant going in motion will have nothing to do with the play. All they are trying to do is to soften the perimeter and then attack you in the area where you have adjusted. Do you know what frustrates them? Either send someone with the motion man, or just sit there and let him go. That really gets the offense frustrated. That blows their mind. They take the 15 play in the game plan that they have scripted for that situation and they throw it out. "That damn play is no good because we didn't get anything out of it. Throw it out of the game plan." They are looking for a lot of movement out of the defense with that motion. If they can get you to move a lot of people on defense with one man going in motion, that is what they want. They want to create confusion for you on defense and soften the perimeter. They know the defense will not play aggressive if they are confused. It is simple. Make sure you set your perimeter and get the adjustments ready and try not to change the perimeter defense if at all possible.

Offensive teams love little or no pressure. How many times do you see the coach that is lecturing on offense show you the play against the Blitz? Do you ever see them draw up a play against pressure? "If they are going to pressure us on offense we have to find a way to get the ball off quick." That is about all they will say about pressure. That statement is damn revolutionary. They damn better sure get rid of the ball fast against the pressure or they are going to get their ass kicked. The do not like pressure. In your multiplicity you must have pressure. That does not mean that you have to run it a lot, but you must have the ability to pressure their butts.

Another thing the offense likes is Rhythm. They love to get the rhythm going. On defense you must have ways to break the rhythm of the offense. You break the rhythm by stemming, by disguising, by stunting, and through multiplicity. You must do something to break their rhythm. You cannot let them come out of the huddle and run against the same defense. If the offense likes rhythm, then you have to have a rhythm breaker. Build your defense with rhythm breakers in mind.

There are a lot of other things to look at on offense such as down and distance and other things that vary week to week. The things I am talking about here are things the offense is looking for against the defense. I am telling you that you better have answers to those things they are looking for because when they get the rhythm you have to get it away from them or you are in trouble.

When you start building a multiple scheme you must do several things. You are trying to find an edge by running the multiple scheme. Let me tell you one thing about multiplicity. Don't get wrapped up in defenses. Don't get so wrapped up in the number of different defensive looks, or the number of different stunts you can run, or how many coverages you can run, and then forget the basis of defensive football. To us the basis of football is having 11 people on defense getting pissed off, getting to the football, and when they get there, they knock their ass off. That is what defense is all about. You can X's and O's yourself out of the game. Defense is built on swarm, pursuit, 11 men getting to the ball, and knocking their ass off. That is your edge. Don't look for the edge in multiplicity. Look for the winning edge by having your people play their asses off. When you get that edge, it does not make a lot of difference what you run. Two or three things will be enough on defense if they get after the offense. Get them to swarm to the football. That is the edge we are fighting for now. That is what we want on defense.

I do not believe in the bend-but-don't-break theory. I do not want to give them an inch. That is not my makeup to give them anything. I have coached the defensive line all of my coaching career. When a defensive lineman backs up when the ball is snapped he is going to catch it from me. This is what I like to tell them. "If you were in World War II fighting for General Patton, and you backed up like that, he would have shot you right in your tracks." We do not want to retreat! We want to attack. I do not want the offense to make an inch. If they make an inch, I am pissed off about it. That is my attitude about defense. I do not get into the theory of bend but don't break. I do not want to depend on the offense to stop themselves. I do not believe it will happen too many times the way the rules are written today. It does not matter if they score on the second play or on the 10th play, it still hurts. So, I do not believe in giving them anything on defense. I want to be an attacking defense. Did I say Blitz? No! I did not say Blitz. I want to be an attacking defense. I want to be able to attack from different angles, different fronts, and different stunts. We want to be always changing angles on the Off Tackle, Isolation, and on the Sweep. That is what you have to have built into your defense.

Very quickly, how are we multiple? I can draw fronts up for you all day, and I will cover a basic front and how we do it later.

As we are building the defense I want to have the ability to adjust. I saw the offensive coaches stand up here and tell us the same thing. They have to have the ability to adjust. If you do not have the ability to adjust and give your kids a chance to play, then you have done a poor job of coaching. Have the ability to make the adjustments that will allow them to win.

Once you have a system that allows you to adjust you must continue to evaluate and reevaluate the defense all of the time. Don't be afraid to do things a little better on defense. I do not believe in the old adage "If it ain't broke, don't fix it." I did not say change. If it ain't broke don't fix it; what do you have to do, wait until you are beat 40–0? Then you can say, "The S.O.B. is broke now; I'd better start fixing the damn defense." The alumni do not want it to be broken before you start fixing the defense. You must be evaluating and re-evaluating how to do it better all of the time.

As you build your defensive scheme I think you need to be unpredict-able. That will give the offense problems. I think you need to be as unpredictable as you can on down and distance, and field position. The offense is looking for the "always situation" from the defense. If they can get you to the point where they can predict what defense you will play on certain situations they will attack you successfully. I will tell our staff that we are never going to always anything. Be unpredictable. Make the offense get wrapped up in ifs. "If they do this, we will do this, etc." If you can do this it will cut down on their ability to scheme and the number of things they can do against you. If they get those always situations, they can game-plan the hell out of you. Build within your system—unpredictability.

Someone asked me when I called a certain defense. I do not know when I called any particular defense. I am sure most of the defensive coaches do the same thing as we do. I can tell you when you call a certain defense. They come out of your damn gut on game day, that is when you call a certain defense. They are not on a piece of paper. That will not get the job done. You call the defenses out of your gut. You study the game plan by the hour. You look at the tendencies. I play the game. John Guy is my roommate on the road. I get up about 5:15 a.m. and get showered and dressed and take a film and sit down by myself and look at the films of our opponents. Do you know what I am doing? I am playing the game. I see the down and distance and I start calling the defense. Then I see the play. I play the game over and over again. By the time I get to the stadium, I will have played our opponent about 4 times. So, when the game starts, the calls on defense have to come from your gut and your instinct.

How do you create uncertainty in an offense? First of all, you can give them different fronts on defense to confuse them. Then you can stem to the different fronts on defense. The no-huddle does not bother us at all. Teams tried that against us this year. We just line up on the ball and our strike makes his call. I call the defense and we signal it in the game. Our linebackers call out our defense as the quarterback is calling their play. We do not have to be set while he is telling his people what to do. We can do the same thing they do, and call our defenses as they call their plays.

Most offenses will come in with something like the no-huddle offense and try to shatter you with it. They will try new wrinkles and if they are not successful with it in a couple of plays they will go to something else. If they have some success they will stay with it.

You can create uncertainty by how you disguise your secondary. You can line them up in a defense that looks like man but is a zone, or it looks like Cover 1, but it is Cover 2. We like to disguise our defense to create uncertainty. That is what we do in building our defense.

I am asked, "How do you coach a multiple defense?" The big question is this: "How do you do all of those things on the multiple defense?" "I do not see how your kids can line up and play all of the different things on defense!" Let me tell you something, this game is not that complicated. I promise you the game is not that complicated. There are three techniques in football. We have a head-up technique, a left shade, and a right shade, and that is it. How you get them over the center, guard, tackle, or end does not make a damn. You have to have names to do that, but those techniques are the same three. When you have a guard playing on the outside shoulder of the guard, it is the same as playing on the outside shoulder of the tackle. You teach your kids to play right shade, left shade, and head up, and you can play any defense you want. You have to have a communication system of how you want them to line up. Those are words. Teach them to play those three positions and they can play it all then. How much they can learn after that to get them into all of those alignments, that will depend on you. Don't make multiplicity any harder than it is, because that is all it is.

If you are going to be multiple you must have a system to call it. I have been a part of multiple defenses since the 1970s, but the way we call our defense is the best system that I have been a part of in that period of time. I did not build this defense, and I did not invent it. I do not take any credit for it at all. I have had some input in building the defense. I think this is a great system, and we have adopted the system. We have built on it, and we have made it even better than what it was in 1984, when we first started using it. I will share with you how we call our multiple defense. It is a system of communication. That is what you must have. In your system you must have a way to communicate the defense to the players so they can get lined up and execute the defense. I will take one front on defense and show you how we can get into about eight different fronts out of a Three-linebacker Stack Defense. It is so simple that it is funny, and I will show you that in just a minute.

The other thing I have heard about the multiple defense is this: "When you do so many different things you give up something, and that is technique." A lot of people will say that repetition is the key to playing football. "Let them play one technique all the time and they will become good at it." That is BS to me. That is a cop-out. You do not have to give up technique when you become multiple. It goes back to what I have said to our players. "A 3 technique on the left, is a 1 technique on the right." We do not give up one ounce of technique to be multiple. If you give up technique to be multiple, it is because you did not coach defense.

We play a lot of Three-linebacker defense. We also play a two-linebacker defense as well. We have trigger terms for our men up front. They have five or six alignments, not techniques, because we know there are only three techniques. Those alignments tell you which man to play one of the techniques on. That is multiplicity. Very quickly let me show you these defenses. This is our base look.

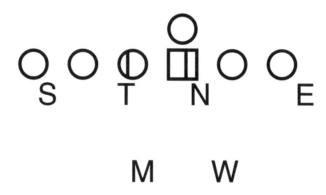

To me this is a 3 stack defense. The base for the nose is a weak shade on the center. Base for the end is a 5 technique on the tackle. The base defense for the tackle is a 4 technique.

When we make a 3 call it tells the tackle to line up in the 3 technique. If we want to move the 3 technique tackle over to a 4 technique we call it a 4 stack. We have moved the tackle over about six inches and we call it a 4 stack. If we call a 4 stack, only the tackle lines up in a 4 technique and plays that technique. No other linemen have that trigger term. On the 4 stack we are lined up inside and keying the guard. The linebacker lines up in a stack and the tackle gets in his 4 technique.

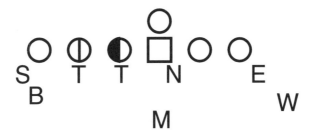

If I want the tackle to line up inside the man and key the tackle, I call 5 stack. That looks the same, but it is not. If we want to send the outside linebacker we just call stack-scrape and the linebacker scrapes in the hole. That is not very hard. If the line does not hear a number called on the defensive alignment, the line knows to get into their basic alignment.

All of this has been called from a noseguard being set on the center which is a form of 50 look. In this defense we have a 3, 4, and 5 stack, and a lion stack, and stack scrape. That is about four or five defenses right there.

If we call 1 tackle stack we line the tackle in a 1 and tackle tells him to take a lateral step out to a 3 technique on the snap of the ball. We are back to playing 3 stack when the ball is snapped.

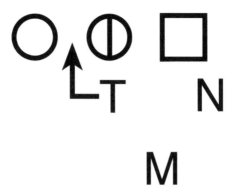

We have shown them one look before the snap of the ball and moved to another look as the ball is snapped. I have given you about five or six defenses with those simple changes. It is a system of communication. This is not the only system, but I think it is a very good system of communications. It allows us to do a lot of things on defense. If I am giving single-digit calls they are always for the tackle. If we give a double digit the first number is for the tackle and the second number is for the nose man.

If you play a three-linebacker defense from an odd look, the offense will have schemes for that look. But let me tell you what makes it tough for them. They have to have a new package when you slide that nose off the center and over to the guard and make the scheme look like an even defense. Rule wise, they have to block it totally different. This is a stack defense and they have to block it differently.

We started from the odd look and now we go to the even look. We call "31 stack." The first number is for the tackle, and the second number is for the guard. The tackle plays the 3 and the nose plays the 1 technique. Everyone else plays his regular stack technique.

If we take the nose and back him off the ball it is a new ball game. They have to have a new set of rules to take care of that look. If we call "13 fire stack" the tackle goes to the 1 technique and the nose is in a 3 technique. Fire tells the tackle and nose to switch gaps on the snap of the ball. On Fire they go from a 1 gap to a 3 gap; or from a 3 gap to a 1 gap, depending on the call.

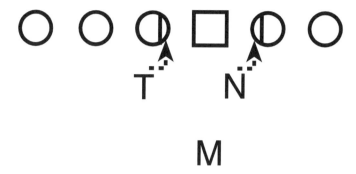

You can see that we can call a lot of different defenses with this system. We have called 3 stack, 4 stack, 5 stack, stack scrape, lion stack, 1 tackle stack, 31 stack, 13 fire stack. Do you want me to keep going? It is like a nuclear reactor. Tell me how complicated is this defense? This is just with one three-linebacker defense. If we call "33 nose stack" we line the nose up in a 3 technique and he fires into the center on the snap of the ball. The nose tells the nose man to fire into the center and we end up in a 31 stack after the ball is snapped.

If we call "11 tackle stack" we line the tackle and nose up in the 1 gaps and on the snap of the ball the tackle fires into a 3 technique. Now, all we are playing is a 31 stack. The tackle call triggers only the tackle.

This is the way we call our defense. I do not know what I am going to call before the game on each play. I do have some idea on what I want to call on certain situations, but it is a gut call most of the time.

Chapter 12

DEFENSIVE LINE TECHNIQUES

Vince Okruch
Northwestern University
1996

What I will do today is go through a format that will cover all the questions you might have. This is identical to what I do with our players each spring and fall.

The first thing I believe is you have to have some kind of philosophy. When I came to Northwestern, the respect we had there was menial. The school had gone through a number of losing seasons. Each year we remind our players that there is a certain amount of respect that they have to earn from their opponents. Our guys had to force the teams in the Big Ten to respect them. We came up with a term called "Respect the Hat." This was a motivational tool. We put a Northwestern helmet on the wall so that each day the players went to practice, they could see that "hat" and know there should be respect sent their way. In order to get the philosophy worked out, we identified five areas we had to improve in:

1) Mental and physical toughness

2) Physical shape and condition

3) Intensity

4) Pride

5) Demanding as coaches

In order to do those things, we felt there were other things to consider. We felt we had to be in great physical condition. It is hard to be tough, intense, or demanding if you are not in shape.

The first thing we did was to start our off-season conditioning. If you are not physically ready to play, none of this other stuff will matter.

I'm not talking about talent. If you looked around the Big Ten you wouldn't find Northwestern at the top as far as talent. Talent has nothing to do with physical condition.

There has to be a great desire to play. I want our defensive linemen to play like their hair is on fire. I don't care whether it is four, eight, or 10 snaps. While they are on the field I want them playing like they are crazy. The best way I found to achieve that is to play more than one guy at a spot. Which would you rather have in a critical situation, a first-teamer who has played 45 or 50 snaps, or a fresh second-teamer? I don't think there is going to be a whole lot of difference.

The other thing we had to change was the attitude. That is the most demanding thing we had to do. There is an old saying that goes, "Whether you think you can or can't, you're right." We inherited a program where there were a lot of bad thoughts. Everyone wanted to look behind. One of the first things Coach Barnett stressed from day one was we were going to look forward.

There are some things the coach and player can do to make this philosophy work. The coach has to be enthusiastic. If you are not happy with what you are doing, you can make a lot more money with the hours you spend doing something else. I can't wait each day to get on the field. I hate sitting in that meeting and film room. I just want to get on the field, get somebody to move the ball, and let things fall where they may. The coach has to transfer that to his players, especially those players who are playing in those trenches. It is tough in there if you are not excited about it. How are they going to get excited about getting hit in the face 65 times in a game? I think the coach has to be demanding. We tell our players if they will allow us, we are going to take them somewhere they couldn't take them-selves. We will force them beyond their normal range of capabilities. The third thing the coach has to be is positive. That is the hardest thing for me. When the score is Notre Dame 45, Northwestern 3, it is hard to be positive. The players are not going out there and intention-ally not doing what you ask them to do. If the coach stays positive, they'll do the best they can to stay positive.

As players, they have to do their job. We have a competitive chart. Anytime we do something competitive, we grade it. It doesn't matter whether it is practice, scrimmage, or game. That is how we measure whether the player is doing his job. I think everyone has had the guy that looks the part. He lifts the weights, runs great times, and looks like a football player. When he gets on the field, you find out he has played a whole game and made one tackle. Then you've got this guy who is 30 pounds underweight, looks like he's never been close to a weight room, and looks bad. But put him on the field and something happens. We play the guys that make something happen. I don't have to answer another question when a guy comes in and wants to know why he is not playing more. All I do is pull out his competitive chart and show it to him. You can use this as an evaluation tool for yourself as well as the player.

We tell our players it is a team game. Up front we are a reduction defense. This defense is as old as they come. We reduce one side or the other. Our defensive linemen try to make plays. But their most important job is to make sure the linebackers can flow to the football. The coach has to convey to the defensive linemen and they have to buy into it. We had a linebacker this year who played nine games, won the award for the nation's best defensive player, and probably not a coach in here would have recruited him. He was our team captain, leader on defense, and does a great job. All we had to do in the defensive line was to make sure the guards and center could not get to the second level. If they don't get there, that linebacker would make the play. Sometimes that meant the noseguard had to sacrifice himself in the double team. Our defensive linemen have to know where they fit in with our scheme of defense. We are not like the Miami Hurricanes, who attack, flatten out, redirect, and make the play. We don't have those kinds of people. I know, if our tackles and noseguard will keep the offensive blocker on or around the line of scrimmage or consume two blocks, our linebacker will make plays.

The players have to be their own unique personality within the team system. I don't want a bunch of robots. About 90 percent of the guys are going to have an earring. That used to fry me. Now if they want to wear an earring, that's okay with me. The new thing now is a tattoo. They wear them on their arms or legs. Who knows what they are going to have cut in their hair or how they are going to trim their face? I don't care. What they have to understand is their unique personality stops at the sideline. When they go onto the field they are part of a team.

There are nine "musts" of defensive line play. We work in phases. My players must understand these things. Let me go through these with you, because this has been my format for teaching everywhere I've been. The first three are grouped together: (1) Alignment; (2) Assignment; and (3) Get-off. These three musts are mental. The "Alignment" is basic to any defense. Without proper alignment, the soundness of the defense goes out the window. The second thing is "Assignment." If we are not moving the defense on a stunt, then our assignment is a shade technique. We are going to play base defense about 85 percent of the time. Understanding the assignment is critical to the defense. The last thing that is mental is the "Get-off." Some guys try to tell me that somebody should have a faster get-off because he is faster. I don't buy that. I tell them there is a string from the end of their nose to the football. When the football moves, that should pull them forward. I believe to be effective on defense, the defensive line has to get off on the snap and go full speed through their responsibility. I spend an awful lot of time on get-off drills. We do it on bags, air, sled, in the chute, moving left and right, and on the ball. I believe that once the ball moves we become an aggressive attacking defense. I don't think you can work it enough. When they start to move slowly, that is a mental thing. They have allowed something else to get into their heads. They are tired or something else.

Those three factors should not determine who plays and who doesn't. Everyone in this room knows his right from his left. We all know a 1 and 3 technique. Everyone knows what coming off the ball full speed is. When the ball moves, they move.

The next three "MUSTS" are ability related: (4) Hand placement; (5) Face placement; (6) Read. These factors can be improved with practice and training. We work a tremendous amount of time on hands in the proper place. We want to work into the pectorals, with our thumbs up, and try to get full extension. I can guarantee if you don't get either hand into the offensive blocker, you are done. If you get one hand in, the defender has a chance. If the defender can get both hands inside, he can control the blocker regardless of the size or strength of that blocker.

The next thing is "Face Placement." When I talk about that, there is some athletic director getting nervous. I know everyone has heard that using the head is wrong because of the neck injuries. I think if you don't teach where to put the face, I think we are wrong as coaches. I have a great drill I'll show you later about face placement. I teach them where their face should fit. They have to keep their face up to see. With the face up, that is the safest position for the neck. When I say work this, we are talking about every day.

The third part is the "Read." This has a lot of ability tied into it. To teach the "Read" we try to give them as many repetitions as we can. We work key drill, half-line drills, and group run situations.

The last three are (7) Escape; (8) Pursuit; and (9) Tackling. We teach that those things are tied into effort. If the defender gets blocked and uses all the techniques he has been taught, there still comes a point in time when the defender has to get off the block and make something happen.

I believe that most of that is effort. I know you guys have coached players who are always around the ball. You are not quite sure how they get off the blocks, but they are always around the ball.

We grade our pursuit in every competitive phase of practice. When I grade pursuit, if one of the down linemen is not in the frame of film when the ball stops, he gets a minus. If he shows up in that frame somewhere, he gets a plus.

We have a 10th "must" we talk about. The bottom line is they have to find a way to win. All the other things will help them win and become a successful lineman, but the ultimate goal is to win the ball game.

Let me go through these nine "musts" in a little more detail. When we talk about "alignment," we talk about stance. We are a three-point stance team. We play with our inside foot back and our inside hand down. If I am on the left side I am in a right-handed stance with my right foot in a heel-to-toes stagger. We believe the strength of the defense is from the belly out. That is why we step with our inside foot and never get turned out. There is always a collision point and we are moving the inside part of our body into whatever shade we have. If we can make you run left and right instead of north and south, we have a chance to run you down.

It is difficult for right-handed guys to play on the left side. We start our right-handed guys in four-point stances until they become comfortable in the left-handed stance. All our drill work is done from a right- and left-handed stance. We feel by doing that we give them the opportunity to play out of a left-handed stance.

Our technique alignment is numbered just like our gaps. The guard-center gap is called the 1 gap. A lot of people call it the A gap. The guard-tackle is the 3 gap. The techniques are 1, 3, or 5, left and right. That is all they have to know.

The next "must" is "assignment." The 3 technique player is responsible for the 3 gap. The 5 technique player has the 5 gap, and the 1 technique player has the 1 gap. We play with a tilted noseguard. That seems to drive centers crazy. I have no idea why, but it does. The noseguard's aiming point is the ear hole of the center's helmet. He is trying to fit himself into the V of the center's neck. The one thing the noseguard has to do is make sure the center does not leave the line of scrimmage. If the center is trying to scoop the noseguard with the backside guard, that can't happen. The noseguard cannot allow the backside guard to take him over. If the backside guard comes off for the linebacker, we feel the linebacker can fight through that. But if the center gets off the noseguard, he can wall the linebacker back. As the ball is snapped the noseguard goes right through the center's ear hole. If the center tries to leave the line of scrimmage, the noseguard holds him there. If he has to, he grabs him. Most of those officials can't see that.

We do all our "get-off" on movement. Anytime you are working any drill, take a football with you. I've tried using an orange football to highlight the ball. I have used a football cut in half so I could keep it with me at all times. I've done lots of things. Use any method you can to get them to come off on the movement of the ball. As the movement of the "get-off" comes, they must start to read the offensive lineman's hat. I want them to see the ball and the snubber on the helmet. The snubber is that area of the helmet where the team name or the maker of the headgear goes. I want to know if the snubber came straight at him, did it go inside like a veer release? Did it take my outside shoulder like a reach block, or did it come straight up like a pass block? Every time you do these drills, take a football with you. If you are going to ask them to move off of that during a game, do it in practice. Moving your foot or a cap is not the same thing.

In the attack phase of our technique we step with the inside foot to avoid being turned out. It also helps us to maintain good leverage. I'll talk about the drills later. When we step and attack, we read on the run. We are moving on the ball and reading the hat of the offensive blocker as we get into our assignments.

On the "hand placement" we want to get into the upper pecs of the offensive blocker. Even though the offensive blocker may have a longer reach, if the defender can get his hands inside first, he can control the blocker. It is that simple. Whoever gets the inside has control.

We talk about "thumbs up." Our strength coaches tell us you have more strength with your thumbs in the turned up position. I fit them on the sled with their thumbs in proper position. We try to get the hand on the pecs, with the thumbs up, and grab cloth. By grabbing the cloth the defender can steer the shoulders. If he can get the blocker's lead shoulder turned there is no back in America who will try to outrun that. If he does, he is not going to gain much ground.

When we teach the "face placement" we are thinking about safety. We want the face placed so that it is up. That is the safest position, and they can see. We have drills to teach the placement of the face. I'll show you those later.

The "read" phase requires a tremendous amount of drilling. There was a coach at Eastern Illinois about 15 years ago who did a study for his doctoral on skills. He went out to Stanford University to do these physiological studies. He found out that when a person does some physical skill, it takes 250,000 repetitions to become familiar with that skill. The shocking part about this is that to master or perfect a skill you must do that skill one million times. We tell our kids that and they think they are going to hit the sled for months nonstop. We are trying to tell them that there is no substitute for repetition. We are very fortunate to have the Chicago Bears headquarters very close to our campus. I have gone up there and watched their practices a number of times. I've watched Chris Zorich. When the first team is not involved in a team drill, he is hitting the sled. He does it over and over again. There is no substitute for repetition. We teach the read with repetition. We are trying to key the hat and tell which way it is going.

The purpose of the get-off, hand placement, head placement, and the read are to gain separation and get off a block. If the defender cannot separate himself from the offensive linemen, he can't make any tackles. Without separation the defender cannot have success. The defender has to get off the block as quickly as he can. We want to escape and make the ball redirect as fast as possible. We like to use the terms "Shed and Spill." When we "Spill," we are going across the ball. When we "Shed," we are going to the ball. It is terminology. If he "Shed," that means he maintained his shade and never crossed the blocker. If he "Spilled," he crossed the blocker. This only helps us in the movement of our linemen when we know what they did.

"Pursuit" is a want-to thing. The thing you can coach is a proper angle to the ball. We do pursuit drills every single day. We want to get all 11 hats to the football. I heard some coach say "a defensive player's importance to his team was directly related to his distance from the ball." That is a very profound statement. That is in my meeting room. It is hard for big guys to do these pursuit drills. That is where the effort comes in.

When we talk about movement we use the term "Rip." All of our movement involves a "Rip Technique." A "Rip Technique" to us is a lateral step, dip, and rip. We want to give our people three ways to go. When we face an opponent we want to be able to move our defenders to the outside or inside or play base. I don't believe you can play an entire football game in base defense and survive. As big as offensive linemen are, you have to move on them. If you don't move on them and keep them on their heels, you will have a long day. We move quite a bit, and it helps us. We don't do it with a slant technique. We do it with a lateral step. We try to maintain our shade technique. We dip our shoulders and rip up with the arm, just like a pass rush. We are working for penetration. When we take our lateral step, the defender wants to key the next offensive linemen. If I'm a 3 technique man, as I take my lateral step to the outside, I want to see the tackle. If the tackle is running away from the defender, he rips through the gap and goes for penetration. He knows the play is coming his way. If the defender takes the lateral step and the tackle is coming down on the scoop, he redirects and pursues the other way. We have a rip and redirect drill that we do about 10-15 minutes a day. We don't do this drill full go every day.

In our practice progression there are three phases. The first phase is a teaching phase. We are in full pads. It is not an off period. It is not a joke-around time, but it is a teaching period. The second phase is a work phase. During this period we hit the sled and do drill work, pursuit drills, and things like that. The intensity during this period goes up. The last phase is a competitive phase. During this period we have scrimmages and high competitive drills. During these periods we want to have a winner. Any competitive phase is filmed and graded. You can't go the whole practice with the teaching phase because it is too low key. You can't go the whole practice with the competitive phase because you would kill them. We work out a practice that is reasonable to accomplish what we want.

One of the things we do for tackling is a little drill with a bag. We use one of those hand-held bags. The dummy holds the bag in front of him to give the tackler a target. The tackler comes toward him. This is not a full-speed drill. It is a half-speed drill to teach tackling. As the tackler gets about a step away from the player being tackled, the player drops the bag. The tackler has to dip, roll his hips, and squeeze that bag. What that does is eliminate the guys from throwing too quick. We were taught not to throw until you could step on his toes. This drill teaches us to get close before they throw. The guys we have to tackle are generally better athletes than the tackler. If we don't get that close we don't have a chance to get a hold on him. We also do like everyone else. We teach the wrap-up, grab cloth, keep the feet moving, and follow through.

The last section of this outline deals with pass rush. We blended some of the 4-3 package into our scheme this year. Our pass rush was so poor, we needed help. Poor is probably too nice a term. We were bad. In pass situations we have gone to an even scheme and a nickel package.

In the pass rush we believe there are two phases. There is the power or bull rush and the speed rush. We teach both kinds of rushes. If we are an outside rusher, about 90 percent of the time we are trying to rush around the corner. We try to beat the fat tackle back to where the quarterback is going to set. We teach our inside guys the power or bull rush. We use a number of moves in their rush technique. We teach a (1) rip, (2) quick rip, (3) swim, (4) quick swim, (5) push/pull, (6) club/counter, and (7) spin/counter. We teach all these moves in training camp. But I know with a guy who is 5'11" and 280 pounds, chances of swimming are not good. He can't get his arm up high enough to make a difference. The same thing is true of a 6'7" guy. He probably can't use the rip move. After we teach all these things, we try to get them to focus in on one move. If you watch the great pass rushers on Sunday, you see them do the same thing over and over again. They do it so well, that they believe the man blocking them can't block them. We want them to focus on one move and a counter for that move. Trying to do all these moves is not productive. They need to master one move and the counter to it. We also tell them in the pass rush, the most important time when they are going to decide what move to use, is when the secondary calls third and eight just as we break the defensive huddle. They can't wait until they get in their stance to decide what pass rush they are going to use. When they know it is a passing situation, they have to decide. If they wait until the snap of the ball, it's too late.

When you scout your opponents this year, put a clock on the quarter-back. Find out how much time it takes him to throw the ball. We found out that if the rusher was going to affect the throw, he has to be in the area of the quarterback in two and a half seconds. If they are not there in three seconds, they don't have a chance. If it takes longer than that, someone is going to come open. What I do each day when we go pass rush with the offensive linemen is take a pass rush. We put a center in the drill to actually snap the ball. When that ball moves, I start the clock. We record the time so that when we watch the tape the next day, we will know if we are getting the job done. That does two things. It forces a sense of urgency. It makes them held accountable for what they are trying to do. What really helped me was the fact that a lot of guys don't realize it is taking them that long to get to the quarterback. They may think they are good pass rushers until you show them the time.

Let me put on a practice schedule and show you how we do this. The first thing we have is a specialty period. I am on the field and our guys can come down and work on anything they want. We stretch for 10 minutes and then go to PATs. The next period is what we call a "Cat Period." During that period we do a strip drill for 10 minutes. I have one guy face another player. One player tackles the other, and the third guy comes in and strips the ball. After that we come together as a defense and do the pursuit drill. The pursuit drill we did this day was the cone drill. We placed cones on the numbers, pitched the ball to one side or the other, and made the defense take proper pursuit angles to the sidelines. We come back in the first drill and do a key drill. The key drill for us is a half-line drill or an inside-3 drill. We take the center and two guards with two tackles and the middle linebacker or a half-line against the one side of the defense. We work good on good. The next thing we to is the "Butt and Bench." That is the face and hand placement drill. We work on stunts and pass rush in the next two periods. The next period we work against the blocking scheme we are going to face. After that we go to 10 minutes of group run. Next we go to 10 minutes of pass rush. We follow that with work against the offensive line. There we work full-line twists. After that, we have a team period followed by a "Pup Period." The Pup stands for "Pass Under Pressure." We work all our blitzes against our offense. We go good on good. We finish up with the team in a scrimmage. That is pretty much how we run our practice.

Let me go through some of our drills. The first drill is our "Get-off drill." We take two guys and put them down in a tilt and 3 technique. I find out the cadence of our opponent that week. Most of the time you can find that out. The defense is required to say a color when they come up and get down. We try and get a key out of the offensive linemen's stance. Our guys can tell sometimes whether a guy is going to pull by the amount of weight he has on his hand. We call "red" for run and "green" for pass. What is amazing is when the 3 technique gives a run call and the tilt gives a pass call, that means we probably are going to get a counter. After they give me the call, they have to go through the appropriate steps. I call the cadence and try to draw them offside by using a hard count. We change sides and tilts to make them get in both right- and left-handed stances. We also do this drill in the cage to keep them low.

To teach players to step with their inside foot, we put them on one knee on a sled. We give them movement and make them contact the sled. They can do it if they don't step with their inside foot. We make them contact the sled with their thumbs up into the pecs area. After we do the drill off one knee, we come back and do it full speed into the sled. They are still stepping with their inside foot and punching out with their hands.

The next drill is the "Butt and Bench Drill." The offense and defense are across from one another on their knees. The offense simply falls forward. The defense has to roll his hips and punch out with his hands. We are checking hand and head placement. Our guys hate to do this drill. All we are trying to do in the beginning is to get him used to headgear coming at him. As the drill goes on, the offense will fall to the left or right of the defense so the defense can see the helmet move as an inside block. This is the teaching phase of the drill. When the offense falls inside and outside, the defense tries to steer the shoulder of the offense. The end of the drill gets their attention. With the defensive man still on his knees, I put the offensive man in a three-point stance and get him to run over the defensive man. They give you a funny look the first time you do this. What it forces the guy on the ground to do is roll his hips and get full extension. If he doesn't, he gets run over.

We use a "Quick-Hands Drill." Sometimes we do it at the start of practice and sometimes at the end. They are getting in a stance and getting their hands from the ground to the pads as quickly as possible. We don't coach hip rotation or punch. We coach quick hands.

Another drill we use to help with the pass rush is the "Hoop Drill." You can make these hoops from electrical conduit or pool vacuum hoses. You need about 18 feet of hose. Make them into a circle. If you use the electrical stuff you will need about three sections. You just lay them on the ground and have your guys run around them. You can make a game out of it. Make them go as fast as they can round the hoop. Make them run figure eights around two of them. What this does is let them practice the speed rush. At some point the rusher has to get to the quarterback. If the offensive lineman backs up, he will run the rusher deep. At some point during the rush the defender has to turn the corner and get to the quarterback. This drill helps him master the turn at the end of the speed rush.

Chapter 13

DEFENSIVE LINE DRILLS AND TECHNIQUES

Joe Sarra
Penn State University
1997

One of the most important things in football is to get the team ready. You have to teach and motivate for a team to perform. The key is to get players to play at the highest level of their ability. We have to push our kids to the point where they don't think they can do it any more. These players don't know what their highest level is because they haven't been pushed that hard. They have to learn to fall down and get back up.

If a player has feet and courage, that is what it takes to be a good defensive player. I ran into one of our players up in the hall before I came down here. He was our manager. We were getting ready to play Notre Dame, and our long snapper got hurt. This manager lined up and long-snapped the ball against Notre Dame for us.

If a kid has courage, you can teach him to be a big hitter. You can make him the best tackler on the team. If you have courage to hit somebody and feet to get to the ball, that's all defense is. If a kid has those talents, it is hard to keep him on the bench.

This next point is important in football but is also important in life's critical situations. You have to *control what you can control.* You can determine whether your team outhustles people. You can determine their getting to the ball. You determine whether your team is in shape. You determine whether your team is in condition. We play two halves of football. The first-half score means nothing. The final score is what counts. You determine whether your team outhits the opponent. We can control the fact that we outprepare people.

151

We control conditioning. In the winter program, if they won't pay the price and condition, they will get you beat on the goal line. They will lose on the goal line. We rate our players in several areas. We consider conditioning, the weight room, academics, and other areas.

When I have a meeting with my players I put on the blackboard, "Today is today. Make it count." However, it's more than that. It is the moment that counts. Any one of us could walk out of here and drop dead. Any tragedy could happen to any of us. You have to cherish the moment.

Here are some things that you build your defense around. You have to be a productive defense. We talk all the time about forcing turnovers. Coach Paterno will come into our meeting and tell us that we need more interceptions and fumble recoveries. We have to force turnovers. The defense must have pride. They have to dominate and defend their area. They have to feel as if no one can run the ball at them. They will defend their area, and no one can run into their area.

We have a saying that is on the board in the linebackers' meeting room: Pay the toll. That is the linebacker area. It is just like the Pennsylvania Turnpike. To use it, you have to pay a toll. Anyone who comes into the linebacker area gets his head knocked off. If a guy crosses the linebacker's face, if he doesn't deck him, he gets a minus-3 on the grading scale. They are to dominate and control their area.

You have to play smart, with poise and pride. They have to have confidence in themselves. There may be a guy with less ability who can play because he is confident that no one can beat him. Toughness is what wins the game. You have to think team, be committed, and be unselfish. Those are things that a lot of people don't have today.

You have to do whatever it takes to win. If you want to win, you have to work harder. People can say that they want to win. That is easy. They have to prepare to win through hard work. You can outhustle people, but execution wins.

This next point is a big one. Coach Paterno does this great. We meet every morning. We look at our personnel board. We move people up and down that board. Who should be moved up a number? Who should we move down? You have to get the proper people in the proper positions. We have moved guys from defense to offense. We had a kid who came to Penn State as a linebacker. Now he is a running back. If you get the proper people in the right positions, they make the plays.

You have to talk to your team. They have to understand your goals and what they are working for. We as coaches are going to work hard but smart. We are working to win. Some people work hard, but they don't work smart.

You have to punish people. You won't win games unless you punish people. You have to get your kids ready to punch somebody in the mouth. You have to get people on the run, and when you get them down, put them away. This is a physical game. We want to beat our opponent physically. How fast you get to the ball only matters if you punish people when you get there. You control gang tackling. It is not how fast you are; it is how physical you are. When the running back is getting pounded, he starts asking the coach to spread the ball around a little.

What are the qualities we look for in the defensive line? The number 1 thing is toughness. I never recommend a guy for our coaches to look at if he is not tough. When I say tough, I mean the tougher the challenge, the better he plays. We want a kid who is a competitor. You won't see size on our list. You can't worry about size. In the line, it is a street fight. You don't talk about weight classes in a street fight. It is the same way with the defensive line. You can't tell the guy that you can't fight him because he is out of your weight class. You can work harder than anybody else to get better. You can go to the weight room and work on your strength. You can work on your hand and foot quickness. The game of football is played with the hands. If you have a guy with quick hands and feet, he can play. We work with martial arts to increase the speed of the hands.

A defensive lineman has to be aware of what is going on around him. He has to shed blockers. He has to be able to change direction effectively. That is important in defensive football. The lineman must stay focused. He has to be able to get off a block. He has to be just downright mean.

In the defensive linemen's meeting room on the left-hand side of the bulletin board is "loyalty and trust." It never comes off the board. We trust each other, and we are very loyal. We never criticize our teammates or talk about them. If I can't trust a player, he is not going in the game. When all the guys are working together, they share that trust in one another. You can't talk out of both sides of your mouth. You have to talk straight.

We evaluate our players. We have a sheet that we use to evaluate them. The strength coach evaluates the players. The trainers and coaches evaluate them. Their academic advisors evaluate them also. We give them a 5, 4, 3, 2, or 1 grade. We want to get the winners on the field. These guys control the tempo of the game. They are the ones who can make big plays and turn the game around. If you have a horse, make sure he gets in the race. Make sure the good back gets his hands on the ball. I'm not talking about some prima donna. I'm talking about guys with character who won't get you beat.

There are three types of guys. There are players who are winners, players who won't get you beat, and players who will get you beat. Forget about potential, and get them to execute. If you have an excuse player, don't play him. He always has an excuse for why he made a mistake. Don't play him. He'll get you beat.

I give our kids a checklist. Defense is our game, and winning is our aim. That is a catch phase for the defensive linemen. I give them a form. On the form are things that we are going to grade and work on all year long. I have the kids grade themselves. I grade them and write down comments for them.

I give them drills to do over the summer to improve on. It is a job description for them. Included on the sheet are the following: change of direction, stance, alignment, assignment, delivery of a blow, shed, pursuit, tackling, and a good base. We also include backpedal, opposite reaction, explosion, read keys, mental alertness, and second effort. I grade the players every night after practice and give them the sheet the next day.

Next are fundamentals. A player has to move and control his feet. He has to shed the high and low blocks. If a person can shed, he can make plays. Some guys can't get off a block. The tackles have to pass-rush, make tackles, pass-react, pursue, and be tough.

I'm going to talk about stance. We use a three-point stance in the defensive line. If I am teaching a young player a stance, I'll put him in a four-point stance. A four-point stance keeps the lineman down. You can't play with your shoulders turned. You want your pads square and your feet under you. A four-point stance helps the kid to do that. We get into a three-point stance, but 98 percent of our weight is on the ground. We have a slight stagger.

In our alignment we play head up, shade inside and outside, nose up, wide or loose alignment, and gap. We key the ball or anything that moves. If anything moves, we are going.

Our responsibility is whatever defensive technique we are in. I'll cover that later. The reaction is to what the defensive lineman sees. He has to see blocking schemes. He must understand his pass-rush lane.

Let's go back to the mechanics of the stance. We don't use a wide base. That will get you in trouble. We want our feet under our hips. I don't say anything about shoulder width. Every kid thinks his shoulders are wider than they are. Good backs run with their feet under the hips. They don't get their feet outside the body. They are skaters. They work within the framework of their hips. When we start to get down, we put our hands on our knees. If I get in a right-handed stance, my right foot is back, and it is my push foot. If I get in a left-handed stance, it is just the opposite. My knees are bent, and I have some weight on my hands: not too much, but just enough. The off hand is close to the ground. We get in the four-point stance and then pick up the other hand. We are a takeoff team. We read on the run. When the ball is snapped, we take off. In our bent-knee position, we get the power angles we want. We step and explode off the ball.

The first thing we tell our linemen is not to get knocked off the ball. If they get knocked off the ball and back into the linebacker, we can't move. If the lineman is in an outside shade on a guard, his inside hand is down. He steps with the inside foot. By stepping with the inside foot, the lineman can keep his outside leg free. If the stagger is too much, it causes the lineman to rise up. It also doesn't allow him to get into the blocker as quickly as having a shorter stagger. We want to get to the blocker quickly, make contact, punch with the opposite hand, and get off the block.

When the offensive blocker rises up to block, we don't rise up. We strike through him. We learn how to use both right- and left-handed stances. We have to play some techniques that require using the opposite hand down. Make your players line up straight. Your feet determine where the lineman lines up.

When we run drills, we film them. We watch the footwork of the linemen. If they don't step with the proper foot, they get a minus-3. That is discipline. We do it one way. I never stand behind the defense when we are practicing. I stand behind the offense. I want to see the defensive linemen's eyes. I want to see what they are seeing.

I want his toes to be straight ahead. I may say, "Feet!" That means they are too wide or too narrow. I could say, "Stagger!" That means his stagger is too big or not big enough. If I say, "Tilt," that means their footwork will cause them to get reached.

We do something differently than a lot of people do. I have done this both ways. It doesn't matter what you call techniques, as long as your players know what you are talking about. We letter our gaps. The center-guard gap is the A gap. The guard-tackle gap is the B gap. The tackle-end gap is the C gap. Outside the tight end is the D gap. Head up the guard would be B. If we want our lineman on the inside eye, that is a B minus. If we want him to straddle the inside leg, that is called tight B. The B plus is the outside eye of the guard. If we get into the B gap, that is called wide B.

We work hard on responsibility. I quiz my players on their assignments. You would be surprised at the number of kids who leave the huddle and don't know the defense or what the snap count is. They don't pay attention in the huddle.

Here is another thing we could talk about anytime. I'm not here to show you alignments, but we'll talk about them. They have to know the alignment, assignment, and reaction. Those things are more important. Never try to tell a kid that the defense will win a game. A scheme is only as good as the players playing it. Execution wins games. The front does not win games.

People ask us about flip-flopping people. We have done both at Penn State. If you don't flip your people, the guy playing on the right gets to play the trap the same way all the time. He uses the same steps and footwork all the time. But if you flip the guy playing the trap, he has to learn both ways, and it adds to the assignments he has to learn. If you flip your people, you have to worry about jumps. If they are flipping, they have to get set in their alignment. If you don't flip, all they have to do is get ready to play. We don't flip our people anymore.

We run a drill about three times a week called "early work." We take our inside people. We work on best and run traps, reach, scoops, and cutoff blocks. We do this drill before practice. After we work on those things, we put the offense and defense together and work seven-on-seven.

Let's get into the practice schedule and what we do on the field. Nothing fancy goes on out there. The first thing we do is stretch. I work with the snappers and kickers, but they do their stretching on their own. We work on our flexibility. The guys may be big, but the game is played with bent knees. I think we take too much time from practice to stretch. I tell them to get stretched out. I don't care when they do it, walking across campus on the way to practice or coming out to practice, but I'm not going to take practice time for them to stretch. You hope they don't do this, but it could happen. A guy gets into a fight. He can't say, "Hey, John, wait five minutes; I've got to stretch and get loose." We get loose during our drill work.

The first drill we do is a bag drill. They step over the bags and stretch. At the end of the bags, I have them do some kind of football-related finish. The first time, I may have them recover a fumble. The second time, I may roll the ball, and they have to pick it up and score. The third time, I may throw the ball to them. The fourth time, they have to tip it to someone else. Then I may have someone there to form tackle. There are all kinds of things that you can do during the warm-up period.

There are ways to recover a fumble. If you are not getting done what you want to get done, keep your players after practice and make them do it right. When you are trying to recover a fumble, never get on your back. Grab the ball, lock it down with the arms, and pull up the knees and hips. When they come in on the ball, if they don't bend their knees, they'll kick the ball. We work on this every day.

You can make your players bend their knees and run quickly over the bags. To teach our kids to bend their knees, we do a drill called hand-touch knee bends. The player gets his butt down and face up, bends his knees, and puts his hands on the ground. We run three or four players at a time. We start them out with their feet straight up the field. You can't push off and have good acceleration and power with your feet out to the side. We start them running. When I yell "touch," they touch their hands to the ground then. They don't run two or three steps and then touch. In a game, your reaction is not when you want it. It is when it occurs. On defense, you have to gain ground on every move. After the touch, they come out low, hard, and accelerating. When a player comes out high, he is not gaining ground. Whatever drill you do, make sure they are gaining ground on the first step. I don't tell them to go. They touch and go.

Every day we do stance-and-starts. We put them in their stance and make them come out low and hard. We tell them which foot to move first. We emphasize elbows in tight and pumping. We are looking for explosion.

We do a grass drill to teach players how to fall. If you feel yourself fall, what do you do? You put your hands down to break your fall. If you fall and want to get up quickly, you use your hands and feet. We teach our kids how to fall. You have to get up on the way down. We do this drill. They start to chop their feet. I say, "hit." They hit the ground, get their hands and feet under them, and come up running. Make them get up and down two to three times and make them tackle to finish the drill. This is the second-effort drill. How many times have you seen guys come off the ground to make tackles, sacks, or recover fumbles? I've seen it lots. If a guy can't give us a second move, he can't play for us.

We use this drill for linebackers and down linemen. The first way we teach this drill is in an up position. We teach them how to slide and change directions. You have to be able to defeat the low block. If you can defeat the low block, you can beat the high block. If you are playing the high block and the low block comes, you can't beat the low block because your legs are split. You cannot shed the low blocker. The feet have to stay under the hips at all times. If the feet get outside the hips, the player can't make a second move. If he keeps his feet under his hips, he can go right, left, forward, or backward. The knees have to be bent, and the back foot must be active in the slide.

In the change-of-direction drill, the toes have to remain straight ahead. If the toes turn, the shoulders turn. We want the pads parallel. We have three guys in the drill. There are six guys behind them in what we call the bull pen. They are practicing the drill. They are moving their arms and practicing. I say, "switch," and the second line becomes the first line and continues the drill. The third line moves up and practices while they wait for the next "switch" call. You don't become a better player by standing around.

The next drill is the lateral run. We don't slide our feet, we cross over. We don't want a big, wide step. It is a short movement like a carioca step. We keep our toes straight up the field as we cross our feet. My butt is low, and my knees are bent. If we turn our feet, the shoulders turn also. We can't shed anybody or change directions if our shoulders and feet are turned. Don't let them rise up when they change directions. If you do, you will get beat. When your eyes see something, they don't tell you to rise up.

This next drill is not a good drill—it is a great drill. We do it every day. We have two long, flat dummies. We have two guys facing each other. One guy is going to his right, and one is going left. They have their hands on the dummies. They slide up and down the dummies. While they are sliding up and down the dummies, they can't take their hands off that bag. When they get to the end of the dummies. they turn and sprint. You can do the same thing with a board instead of a dummy. The main thing is to make them move laterally and keep their hands down.

We take the drill one step further. We have an offensive player and a defensive player. They do the same drill, but as they get to the end of the bag, the offensive player tries to cut the defensive player with a low block. The blocker is trying to get to the knees of the defensive player. The defensive player has to keep his hands down and shed the blocker. If the defensive player gets to the end of the dummy and rises up, he is blocked. We work on movement, shedding, and keeping down. We slide down with the toes straight and then cross over with the toes straight, always keeping our hands on the bags. It makes them bend their knees and stay down.

We look hard in our game films for guys who do these drills in actual game situations. This drill is one you can find all the time. That is why it is so good. We set up a series of bags and make the linemen step over the bags using the form they worked on in the hands-down drill. They step over the bags going right and left. At the end of the bags to the right and left, we have a tackling lane with a ball carrier. We go through movement, change direction, see the ball carrier, explode up into the lane, and make the tackle.

This next drill is a million-dollar drill that you can get on credit. Go down to the hardware store. Buy some rubber tubing, and make a circle. Even when you pass-rush, you have to maintain good body position. We put two guys across the circle from one another, one in a right-handed stance and one in a left-handed stance. On movement, they run around the circle. They have to keep the hands down on the tubing. They have to lean to stay on the circle. The head is up, and the knees bent. When they get all the way around, they change directions and go the other way. This gives them the idea about coming around the horn in the pass rush. It teaches them to lean in and make the play on the quarterback instead of running past him.

Chapter 14

DEFENSIVE LINE TECHNIQUES

Jim Tanara
Eastern Kentucky University
1995

I want to teach you a little about the defensive front and how we do things at Eastern Kentucky University. I coached the old 50 defense until about 1991. That is when I switched over to the 4-3 defense. That was hard for me because I was the type of defensive coach that kept all the linebackers free. I taught stepping with the inside foot and squeezing down. Now that I have gone to the 4-3 concept, all we do is line up and get after people's rear ends. The first year I taught that, it was horrendous. The more I'm around the scheme, the more I like it.

We take speed and athletic ability over size all the time. That is within reason. I know you can't play with a 145-pound defensive tackle. Some of the things I'm going to talk about will be a natural for guys with athletic ability. For someone who doesn't have athletic ability, they have to be technique perfect.

Never ask your players to do something they can't do. If you want a 2 gap player to line head up, whip the offense, and then play the gaps right and left, you better have a big physical guy. That is one of the reasons we went away from the 50 defense. We couldn't find those guys. When you get in a shade technique, I can talk to my guys about whipping half the man. That is what I like about the one-gap scheme. Basically we see the same blocking schemes all the time regardless of what we play. In high school, where you have to play anybody that shows up, you should consider this scheme. If you line your guys up and send them to the right or left, that is about the same thing. But if you are making that guy read, whip the man in front of him and play two gaps, you may be asking him to do something he can't. If you have an athlete with skill, put him in an alignment where he can be successful.

One other thing I try to get across to kids is to be physically tough. Mike Tyson said it the best. They told him Michael Spinks had a game plan for him. He was going to keep him away with his jab and keep moving. Mike said, "Everyone has a game plan until they get hit." That is about the truth. You have to win the physical battle up front. If you can win the battle up front, you have a chance to win the game. We have a player on our team right now that doesn't have a whole lot of athletic ability. But, he was a hitter and would get after you. We won a lot of games because of him. It wasn't his ability, but he was technique perfect.

When I was trying to decide what I was going to talk about and how I was going to present it, I got confused. There are so many schemes that I didn't know how to present the material. But all defenses come down to the basic point of whipping a guy and making a play. Those fundamentals are the same regardless of the scheme you use. That is what I want to talk about.

What I teach my kids, talk to them about, and drill them on came down to three areas. Those areas were stance, playing with your hands, and footwork. If our kids got blocked or were not successful, it was usually related to one of those areas or all of the areas. That is why I coach from the very first day to the last day about stance, hands, and footwork.

Stance is a difficult thing to talk to a kid about where they think it is important to them. We line up as close to the offensive man as we can get. There is no margin for error. If I am a linebacker or defensive back, I can make some adjustments before I have to make contact. When the defensive linemen aligns, he better start off right. I've seen a lot of players get whipped before the ball was even snapped because they were aligned so poorly in the stance. They got blocked because their stance was so bad they couldn't get out of it. A lot of times it is hard to get young kids to understand that. What I try to sell them on is the closer you get to the line of scrimmage, the more important your stance becomes.

I think it is easier to get in a good three-point stance than it is to get in a good four-point stance. In a four-point stance everything on both sides of your body has to line up. Some of these guys can't physically get in a four-point stance. It takes a good athlete to get in a good four-point stance. I coached the four-point stance up until 1991, but I had the luxury of recruiting some athletes where you don't. If I were coaching a high school, I would put my defensive line in a three-point stance. I know I can start them out right because I can get them in a good three-point stance.

When I start talking to my kids about stance, I line everything straight down the field. Their shoulders, hips, feet, and everything else is straight down the field. If my left hand goes down, my left foot goes back. The left hand comes straight down. Here are some common mistakes your kids will make getting into a stance. Rather then drop the hand straight down they put it in the middle. That throws their body and footwork off. That is the first thing you look at. We don't want a wide base. We want the feet up underneath in the stance. Not even as wide as shoulders' width. We want the shoulders square. I always let the opposite arm hang. I don't want the shoulders tilted. By hanging the arm, that brings the shoulders square. Don't ask a kid to raise his head to look at the offensive linemen. If he does, his tail will go down. If he wants to look at something, he turns his head. He does not raise it back. That is important because if the head is up his first step is going to be straight up. I have to make that correction all the time. From day one to the last day I am still working on head position. The stagger of the feet depends on the body build of the guys.

The only way a defensive lineman can escape from a block is by using his hands. He has to play with his hands. When we line up in our 4-3 alignment, we are not lined on half a man. We are wider than that. We are on the tip of the offensive lineman. The reason we do that is to make it almost impossible for the linemen to reach block our people. Playing with our hands is extremely important. Everything we do is with our hands. All offensive linemen cheat. They are going to hold. We never use that as an excuse for not doing the job. We keep our outside hand free at all times. The inside hand goes to the offensive lineman's breast. The head of the defensive player goes for the V in the neck looking over his shoulder. We are looking over the collar bone. The coaching point is to "look your hands onto the blocker." If they do that they are looking at the blocker. We want to take first things first. They have to whip the blocker first, then go make the play. The first thing high school kids want to do is raise up and find the ball.

After the defender gets his hands on the blocker, he has to get separation. The description we use is don't get alligator arms. That means real short arms. Get extension in the arm. Don't let the offensive blocker get his hands on you. If your kids are having a hard time playing with their hands here is what you do. You line up with no gear except the headgear and play full speed. I guarantee that makes them play with their hands. Days we are out in shorts and headgear, I have full-speed blocking drills. We don't get anybody hurt. We may get a bruise or so, but no one gets hurt. You will be surprised with what happens with your kids if you do this.

In our scheme of defense the first step we take is straight up the field. The second step adjusts to the blocking scheme. Straight up the field means straight. There are "No Angles" in the first step. The shade hand should be down on the ground. That means the first step is with the foot that is back. The right-side players play with their left hands down. If you have a guy who is making all kinds of plays, it doesn't matter which hand he puts down. As long as he makes plays, I could care less. You will be surprised that some kids can do a good job with either hand down. But if a guy is getting into a bad stance let him put down either hand to get into the good stance.

One thing I want to do on all blocks is to attack the blocker. That means get off the ball. All you guys have heard that old expression that "Low Man Wins." That is exactly the truth. I don't care whether it is in junior high school or the NFL. If the defense gets off the football and is low it wins most of the time. Look at your film. Guys that set on the line of scrimmage get blocked all the time. My coaching point is to attack the outside half of the blocker with your eyes, hands, and feet. I like for our guys to look in for the ball so they get off on the ball. The first step is a power step to balance the defender. His second step adjusts to the blocking scheme. If the blocker goes down, the defender squeezes to the inside and spills any trap block coming.

When you get into the shade defense, you only see certain blocks. The blocks that you see are double-team, reach, turnout, spill, and scoop. The spill to me is a trap block.

We do not see a lot of true double teams. What we see are two guys trying to knock us back into linebackers and one coming off for the linebacker. We see two guys trying to get one guy down the line of scrimmage with one coming off for a linebacker. We don't see a true double-team where two guys are blocking one man. The only time I see that is in short yardage and goal line. When we get this scheme, the first step is always the same. Straight up the field and attack the offensive blocker hard. I don't want the outside man to knock me back or down the line. When I see the outside man coming on me, I drop my head and outside shoulder to the ground. I look like an ostrich. After that I take the shoulder and take out the outside blocker's inside leg. When I do that, I crawl a yard deep in the backfield. If I get the true double-team, I want to do two things. I don't want to get knocked off the ball and I want to occupy two guys. If he can do that, he has done a hell of a job. If that guys can somehow get penetration he can make the tackle. Most teams coach to run over the double-team.

What we see I call "Chip-and-Slip Block." The guard and tackle come off together and engage the defensive tackle. The guard is the primary blocker with the tackle coming off for the linebacker. That is what I call a "Chip Block." If the opposite thing occurs with the tackle as the primary blocker on the defensive tackle and the guard coming off for the linebacker, that is the "Slip Block." We use the same technique on both blocks. The first step is a straight attack step up the field. When the tackle sees the offensive tackle coming down on him, he drops his outside shoulder underneath the blocker and drives into him. The important thing is to get under the blocker. We want the down block to go over the top of the defense. If the tackle releases and goes for the linebacker, the defensive tackle can make the play.

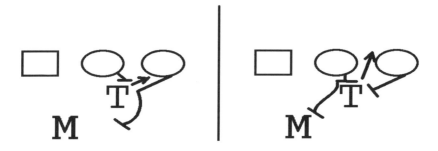

The success of that block has a lot to do with the Mike linebacker. If the Mike linebacker fills and attacks the line of scrimmage, the tackle or guard doesn't have the time to double on the tackle. One of them has to release or they will never get the linebacker. If the Mike linebacker doesn't react, the offensive tackle will stay on the defensive tackle longer and make it tougher. We find that most teams don't do a good job of jamming the defensive tackle with the outside block any way. The blocker's eyes are on the linebacker because that is his block. He is in a hurry to get off to get to the linebacker. For that reason we don't go down on the ground like we would in the true double team. In fact if the tackle chips up to the linebacker and the defensive tackle doesn't make the play, that is a minus for him on the grading system.

The next block is the "Turnout Block." A turnout block to me is when the blocker puts his head inside on the defensive man. I know right now, if the blocker's head is inside, so is the ball. All we want to do on the turnout is to get upfield and restrict the inside running lane. The good thing about getting upfield is the back can't bounce the ball outside. If the end sets on the line of scrimmage and gets the turnout block, the back can bounce the ball and run right by the end. We want our players getting a yard to 2 yards up the field. If the ball stays inside, the end turns, retraces his steps, and makes the play. He only does that after the threat of the bounce and cutback are gone.

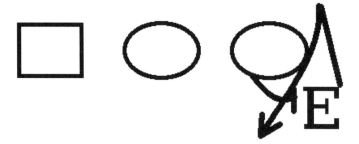

The reach block is the common block people depend on. The first thing I tell my guys is, if that ever happens to them, they are not going to heaven. It should never happen, but it does. If a man gets reached, it's usually the defensive man not looking his hands on the blocker or he is stepping inside. If he looks his hand on the man that is blocking him and steps straight up field, he should never be reached. The offensive blocker to reach has to open up. When he does that he loses all his power and we run right through it. If the offense does gain leverage, we don't retreat or give ground. We are going to press the block and continue to try to run through it. If he retreats, he cuts off the linebacker. I grade my guys every play. If one of them gets reached, that is a double minus. We try to get across to our guys, if one guy blocks them, they are in the wrong business. To block us we want the offense to have to double team.

We get a lot of scoop blocking schemes. Teams usually try to scoop our defensive tackles. The technique we use is to get between the blocker and press on the scoop man. We want to get our feet to next nearest lineman. If the center is leading on the shade tackle with the backside guard coming for the scoop, the tackle gets between the center and guard and presses on the guard. He wants to get his feet to the onside guard. We don't worry about the center because he is trying to get off for the backside linebacker. We see this all the time and I work on it all the time. The tackles spend 70 percent of their drill work time on the scoop scheme.

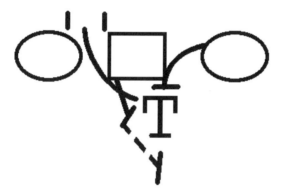

The "Spill Block" to me is no different than a trap block. All kick-out blocks are spilled to the outside with a wrong-arm technique. I like that because it kicks the play outside and our linebacker can make the play. When we spill, it is the only time we turn our shoulders to the line of scrimmage. The rest of the time we want to play with our shoulders square to the line. The defense is coached to know if the offensive man goes inside someone is going to trap his ass. That is the first thing he thinks about. The first step straight up the field doesn't put us in very good position to play a trap.

The second step has got to be down the line. The way we teach it is to "Punch the Hip." That means when the blocker goes down, the defender takes his outside hand and tries to punch him in the hip. He can't do it but it turns his hips and shoulder in to play the trap. The end probably sees the fullback while the tackle sees the guard. When we spill, we want it deep in the backfield. We don't want to sit on the line of scrimmage and spill anyone. The thing that is hard is the offense slams the defensive end with the tight end. The tight end slams and releases for the linebacker. The fullback comes and kicks out on the end. That is hard to play. The way we play this is to attack the tight end so he has a hard time getting off to block any one. Instead of the tight end slamming our defensive end, the defensive end slams the tight end. When we spill we want to attack the trapper. Don't stop and wait for the trapper.

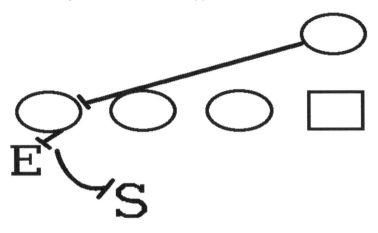

The play that can hurt the 4-3 defense is the "Buck Trap Middle." It hits so quick that all the 3 technique tackle can do once he feels the trap coming is throw his body back into the hole. The thing we do to help is bring the backside tackle to a backside shade on the center. That helps squeeze the play. The man responsible for the trap middle is the Mike linebacker. All the tackles can do to help is keep the hole as tight as possible.

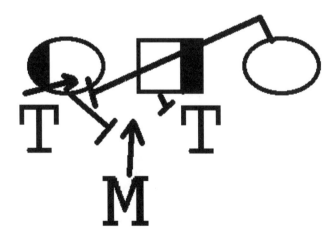

There are three techniques that your kids have to learn as defensive linemen. They have to learn the "Skin, Rip, and Quick Move." They need to learn these things because that is what they do so many times. A "Skin" technique to me is a directional technique. When you line a kid up and slant him right or left is a "Skin" technique. From the shade technique we back up off the ball six inches. That is to get the defense across the face of the blocker. If you are in a head-up position, don't back up. If I am going left, I mentally shift my weight to my right foot. The first step is a flat step to the line of scrimmage and the right shoulder dips. The second step is up the field and the right arm rips through the face of the blocker. The reason we take the flat step is to keep us from getting pushed down the line of scrimmage. The skin move is used to beat a reach or turnout block. If the defensive man takes his lateral step and the blocker blocks down, he lets him go and comes right off his ass to the inside.

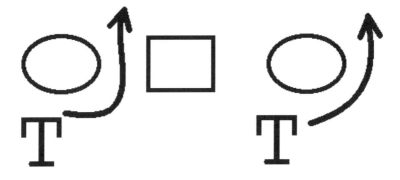

Chapter 15

BUCKEYE DEFENSIVE LINE PLAY

Bill Young
Ohio State University
1992

My objective is to share with you specific techniques and strategies of the defensive line at Ohio State University. I've been the Defensive Coordinator and Defensive Line Coach at OSU for the past four years. Two years ago we changed our defensive line play from a flat-footed read-and-react form of play (or mirror the offensive lineman) to a very aggressive, attack and read-on-the-run style of play. Of the different changes we've made with our defense, I believe this was the single most important one.

Basically we want to be complex but not complicated. Communication is a cornerstone for our defense. We stress it in everything we do. We name every defensive position. Naming enables every player to know exactly who we are talking to when making corrections in meetings, at practice, and during games. We number each technique and letter every gap on the offensive front. We use key words in our defensive calls to alert the significant players of their involvement in a stunt or change-up in technique. For example, our base defense is Eagle, a change-up defense is Eagle T. The "T" alerts the defensive tackle to play a 2 technique as opposed to a 3 technique in Eagle.

Another example is Eagle Ed. That is a change-up for the End. The end now plays a 3 technique, as opposed to a 5 in the Eagle defense. We want to be as complex as possible, giving our opponents different looks to block, yet keeping things simple. Defense is a game of reaction. The less our players have to think, the more effective they become.

We teach and demand our players to give great effort, to hit, to line up right, and to take great pursuit angles. Our players study film of

EAGLE

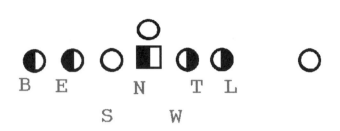

EAGLE T

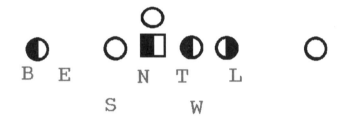

EAGLE ED

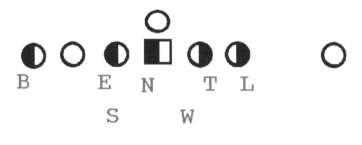

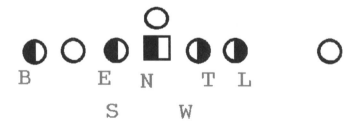

our opponents. In fact, we've gone as far as making personal video tapes for players to take with them to study, along with very involved scouting reports.

We believe our opponents' offense will tell us a lot if we will just listen. Areas of special importance to our defensive players, especially our defensive linemen, are what we call "Presnap Reads:"

1. Time on Clock

2. Score

3. Personnel

4. Down and Distance

5. Vertical Field Position

6. Horizontal Field Position

7. Formation

8. Line Splits/Receiver Splits

9. Stances

The time left in the game, or the half, will dictate a lot toward the tempo and play selection of the opponent. Obviously, the score will have a great influence in the play selection and what to anticipate from the opposition. The personnel in the game is key to the type of plays to expect. When a team gets into a one-back offense and the remaining back is a Fullback, it's generally going to be a pass. However, if the remaining back is a Tailback, it'll be a run because he is a better runner than blocker. We really stress the down and distance tendency of each team we play. We use a computer to break down our opponents' film, and pass this information to our players so they will anticipate plays in certain situations. The vertical field position is also important in knowing what to expect from opponents. Backed up to their own goal line, most teams are conservative, not wanting to give up a turnover. With the ball between the 30s, however, most teams will really open up their offense. We call this the Alumni Zone. Alumni always get excited about trick plays, reverses, and such. Opponents generally become more conservative as they move into field-goal range.

Every team is different. Therefore, we keep a vertical field position by down and distance chart in our defensive meeting room. This chart becomes part of the scouting report we give our players. Horizontal field position is a strong key. We always want to defend the wide field and force the opposition into the boundary as our 12th man. The offensive formations are a vital form of information to us. If a Defensive End sees Trips and a Back offset to his side, he expects a Sprint-Out Pass and aligns a little wider.

There is one team we play that on third and long if they get into the I, your ends had better move in and get ready to squeeze the Draw. If your ends stay out wide and rush upfield, this team will gash you. We played a team a couple of years ago that got into a Halfback offset to Twins. When the fullback aligned behind the tackle it was a run, with the fullback being the lead blocker. If the tailback was offset, it was a sure pass. The tailback would release and run a pass route, and the fullback would be a blocker. It seems the more formations a team runs, the more solid its tendencies become.

It's imperative that defensive linemen are alert to line splits. As a general rule, teams pack it in tight to run outside or pass. If they take big splits, they tend to run up inside. Often, teams will oversplit the middle or guard Center Gap to run the Trap, and oversplit one tackle to run the Cutback.

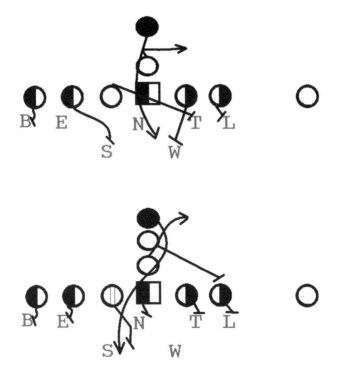

Tight wide receiver splits tell you to be alert for the reverse or Crackback. A defensive back should be thinking about the possibility of an Outcut. Probably the biggest tip-offs of all are the stances of the offensive linemen.

It seems each year the offensive linemen get bigger and bigger. It used to be rare for a team to have a 300-pound tackle. Today, not only are both tackles that big, but several of the guards are, too. Because of their size, they really cheat their stances. If their weight is back on their haunches, we think pass or pull. If their weight is forward, we think run. We work hard to communicate this to our defensive front. If both sides are showing pass, we anticipate pass or draw. If one side shows pass and the other shows run, there is a great chance they are running the Counter Sweep to the run stances side, and pulling the other side.

The center's feet are another good solid key for us. I can't tell you how many teams we played that have had their center up on his toes or running plays and flat-footed on passes. Even more telling, have his off-hand down in a four-point stance on runs and his hand on his knee on pass plays.

In coaching the defensive line, everything starts with the stance. We use four basic types: a Take-Charge Stance, a Move Stance, a Rush Stance, and a Short-Yardage Stance (or Goal-Line Stance). The Take-Charge Stance is used on normal downs in our base defenses. It is a three-point stance with the free hand hanging and ready to deliver a blow. We want our feet armpit wide with 40 percent of our weight on the balls of our feet and the remaining 60 percent of our weight on the down hand. We used to teach it shoulders' width apart, but our players had a misconception of just how broad their shoulders were. It's better to be too tight than too wide. The down hand should be four to six inches out in front of the head gear, with the hips a little higher than the head and the elbow flexed. The whole body is coiled, ready to explode and attack.

The Move Stance is used on defenses which require defensive linemen to slant, angle, rip, or jump around on the snap. This stance looks exactly like the Take-Charge Stance except the lineman must shift his weight to 40 percent on his down hand and 60 percent on the balls of the feet. Mentally, the majority of the weight should be on the foot opposite the direction of the move.

The Rush Stance is used in obvious passing downs. This requires not only a change in stance, but also in attitude. On a Take-Charge and

Move Stance, we are thinking run first and react to the pass. However, on the Rush Stance, we are thinking pass first and then reacting to the run. We want a three-point stance, but we want to elongate it by moving the hand a little out in front of the head and increasing the distance, or stagger, between the feet to about one foot. We also want to move the width of the feet closer together, much like a sprinter in starting blocks. The fourth type of stance is our Short-Yardage or Goal-Line Stance. We want to be in a low, four-point stance, with our weight shifted to 70 percent on our hands and 30 percent on our feet. Our hips are slightly higher than our head, our bodies are flexed, or coiled, ready to penetrate and create a new line of scrimmage.

We teach our defensive linemen to move on movement. We key the ball, the offensive linemen and the quarterback's feet. We want to attack on movement. All of our drill work, even our after practice conditioning, is done on sight not sound. Before we changed from a flat-footed, read of keeping the offensive linemen off the linebackers at-all-cost style to our present attack, read-on-the-run style of defense, we went so far as to grab the offside armpit of the center or guard on scoop blocks and tackled him to free up the linebackers.

OLD WAY: KEPT CENTER OFF LINEBACKER

NOW: WE RUN OFF THE CENTER'S BUTT AND MAKE THE TACKLE

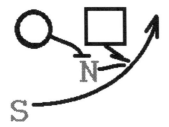
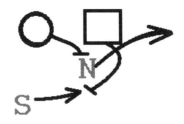

Becoming an attacking defensive line is the best thing we have done. Our sacks have doubled and our tackles for losses have tripled. Although our linebackers occasionally get cut, we think it's worth the trade-off. We instruct our defensive linemen *to avoid being scooped* if the man they are aligned on gets off on the linebacker, and to *make the play*.

In summation, defensively, we believe in good, sound fundamentals. We instruct our players to take care of the "Little Things," teach them to analyze game film, and to study scouting reports. In short: *Prepare To Win*.

About the Editor

Earl Browning, the editor of the By the Experts Series, is a native of Logan, West Virginia. He currently serves as president of Telecoach, Inc.—an organization that conducts football clinics and produces the Coach of the Year Football Manuals. A 1958 graduate of Marshall University, he earned his M.Ed. and Rank I from the University of Louisville. From 1958 to 1975, he coached football at various Louisville-area high schools. Among the honors he has been accorded are his appointments to the National Football Foundations and the College Hall of Fame Advisory Committee on moving the museum to South Bend, Indiana.